TONY

SCANNERS
A VHF/UHF Listener's Guide

Dedicated to

My family. Val, Arron and James for their long suffering patience whilst I was locked away for months in the garret beating the daylights out of the word processor.

SCANNERS
A VHF/UHF Listener's Guide

Peter Rouse GU1DKD

ARGUS BOOKS

Argus Books
Wolsey House
Wolsey Road
Hemel Hempstead
Hertfordshire HP2 4SS
England

First published by Argus Books 1986
© Peter Rouse, 1986
Second Edition 1987
Reprinted 1988 (twice)

ISBN 0 85242 943 6

Phototypesetting by En to En, Tunbridge Wells
Printed and bound by Whitstable Litho Printers Ltd.,
Whitstable, Kent

Contents

1 Introduction   1

A caution. The legal position. Licences.

2 A basic understanding of radio   5

Receivers and transmitters. Frequency/wavelength/spectrum. Distances. Modes of modulation. Channelising. Types of transmission. Simplex/duplex operation.

3 The hardware   22

Crystal controlled scanners. Synthesised scanners. Frequency coverage. Strange switches and knobs. Inputs and outputs.

4 Operating your scanner   35

Synthesised scanners. Base stations. Mobile operation. Portables. Choosing crystals. Using a portable. Interference. Scanner tricks.

5 Aerials   47

Forget the telescopic. VHF/UHF aerials. Narrow band aerials. Broadband aerials. Aerials for portables. Satellite aerials. Cable. Building an aerial. Mounting external aerials. Aerial amplifiers

6 Accessories   67

Power supplies. Loudspeakers/headphones. Computer interfacing. Frequency converters. Miscellaneous.

7 UK frequency allocations   77

Aeronautical bands. Marine band. Amateur bands. Land mobile services. Space satellites.

8   RT procedure   117

Phonetic alphabet. Time. Amateurs. International Q-codes. Marine.
Aviation.

9   Scanner and accessories review   133

A look at some of the equipment currently available in the UK.
Buying guide. Accessories. Antennae.

10   Main importers/manufacturers/agents   165

11   The next stage — Scanners 2   168

     Index   174

Acknowledgements

Clearly no book that includes such a vast range of information can be put together without considerable help from a large number of people. It would be impossible for me to name all the individuals and dealers but I hope they will accept my thanks for their assistance, even if it was merely a morsel of information given in a telephone conversation.

Some people though did provide help beyond the call of duty. They are:

Eric Le Cornu of Jersey whose persistent questions prompted the book.

Richard Bird of Links Communications in Guernsey who guided me on the contents and loaned various items for assessment and photographing.

John Wilson and Lowe Electronics for much speedy and helpful assistance.

Graham Jackson of the Camera Centre, Guernsey, for producing prints from my awful negatives.

Vince and Dave for help with the sections on air traffic control.

Introduction 1

Scanning receivers are sophisticated radios capable of skipping through a series of radio channels and picking up transmissions that cannot usually be found on an ordinary radio. Throughout the world scanner users are tuning in to marine and aircraft bands, monitoring messages from emergency services and the military. It is even possible to tune in to transmissions from space satellites.

But how do the authorities view this activity?
Which scanners cover what frequencies?
Who transmits on what bands?
How far do transmissions carry?
How do you get the best performance?
Which are the best aerials to use?

If you are thinking of buying a scanner, or already own one but cannot answer one or more of the above questions, then read on.

Caution

The aim of this book is to provide a basic understanding of the use of scanning receivers and VHF/UHF communications. Contrary to popular belief this type of equipment is *not* solely purchased by people who have no legitimate right to listen in to certain kinds of radio traffic and who wish to illegally snoop on other people's messages. Many people from amateurs to commercial and professional users buy this type of equipment for perfectly legitimate reasons. However, such people may still not fully understand how to use the scanner to its best ability. This book is aimed at all scanner users who want a better understanding of how their equipment works. In order to achieve that aim it has been necessary to include a wide range of information, some of which might be considered sensitive. I must stress that although certain bands and frequency allocations are shown, the book should *not* be interpreted as an invitation to listen-in — unless the appropriate licence or authority is held.

To sum up: *The responsibility lies with the equipment owner to satisfy himself that he has a legal right to listen-in to any radio transmission.* All information published here has been published before at some time, much of it by the Government. However its publication here must not be interpreted as some kind of right to listen-in. The unlicensed user will find the following information useful.

The legal position

The very existence of scanning receivers has been shrouded with some controversy and, indeed, some countries are planning to ban their sale except to professional or licensed users. Governments have become increasingly worried because use of a scanner clearly enables anyone to tune into transmissions of possibly sensitive natures (police and military being typical examples).

But what is the law? It varies from country to country and clearly it is beyond the scope of this book to provide a global definition. In the USA legislation even varies from state to state. It may be quite legal to listen in to police transmissions in one state but an offence to do so in the next. Some states allow listening-in on a portable or base station but not in a moving vehicle.

What about Britain? In England, Scotland, Wales, Northern Ireland, the Isle of Man and the Channel Islands the relevant law is the Wireless Telegraphy Act and its various amendments. Put simply, the Act says that members of the public are entitled to listen to only two kinds of broadcast; licensed broadcast stations (ie, BBC, Local Radio or foreign equivalents, etc) or licensed radio amateurs. In this respect, it is an offence to listen-in to any other broadcasts

There is a myth that says you can listen-in to anything as long as you do not act on information received or pass on to someone else the contents of any transmission heard. But be warned that this is not so and there have been instances where courts have fined people who have been caught listening-in to police transmissions.

As for scanner users in other countries they are well advised to get advice on their local legal position.

Licences

Having warned about the possible consequences of tuning in to transmissions other than amateur or broadcast it should be stated that licences *are* available to listen-in to, and indeed transmit on, certain frequencies. The most notable are amateur, marine, aviation and Citizens band (CB) licences but it should be stressed that with the exception of CB, licences are only issued to people who have passed relevant examinations. In the case of marine and aircraft these examinations are based on operation and radio procedure rather than technical knowledge. In the case of the amateur licence, however, a basic knowledge of electronics is also required. Information on these licences is available from the following bodies:

Any Post Office (CB).
Any CAA Approved Flying School.
Department of Trade and Industry (Marine).
Radio Society of Great Britain (Amateur).

This book is aimed primarily at the non-technical user of scanner receivers and so, for the most part, tries to explain in non-technical terms how to get the best out of such receivers. However, much of the tabulated data and charts should also provide a useful reference to the more experienced scanner user who I hope will not be offended if he finds other parts of the book 'talking down' to him.

It is difficult to define just when scanning receivers first appeared on the UK market. Certainly the first one I ever saw was in the mid seventies and it was a ten channel aircraft band receiver marketed by the Regency Company of the USA. Shortly after I saw the Tandy Corporation offering scanners to cover police and amateur frequencies in the USA. Not long after that similar receivers for the marine bands appeared followed by the fully synthesised equipment produced by Elektra, who made the Bearcat series.

Next came the second generation scanners led by the now famous SX-200 produced by JIL of Japan. This offered a far greater range of frequencies and modes and has recently been joined by the SX-400 with even greater facilities — it can even be controlled externally by a computer. Now some highly sophisticated machines are available including the ARC 2001/2002 and models by Yaesu-Musen and Icom who are both well known for high quality amateur radio equipment.

As to the future, it seems safe to predict developments in three main areas. First, synthesised hand-held scanners will almost certainly start to offer greater frequency coverage.

Second, optional computer control will become the norm rather than the exception. As you will discover in this book, even a simple home computer connected to a scanner can increase its capabilities by enormous margins.

Third, some VHF/UHF communication users will resort to scrambling and similar methods in attempts to prevent eavesdropping on their messages. Some police forces are already experimenting with digital data transmissions; in which sensitive messages are typed into a keyboard at the base station, converted into digital form and transmitted to appear on a small screen in the patrol car. It is likely that enterprising electronics engineers will follow with equipment to descramble/decode such messages. It seems to be the way of the world these days that the authorities merely resign themselves to trying to stay one step ahead.

As for that ban on scanner sales I doubt now if it will ever happen in the UK. Things have gone too far and such a ban would merely lead to back-door imports of the type seen during the illegal AM Citizens' band radio boom.

The scanner is here to stay.

A basic understanding of radio 2

One question frequently asked by first time scanner buyers is 'how far away from stations can I be in order to still pick up the signals?'. This is a bit like asking 'how long is a piece of string?'. Radio signals are transmitted in different ways and, at the frequencies covered by most scanners, the signals are greatly affected by a number of factors including:

The frequency used.
The time of year.
The aerial used.
The location of the scanner.
The location of the transmitting station.
The weather.

To understand why these factors affect range you need to have a basic understanding of the way radio signals travel. If you are prepared to try and understand the basics in simple layman's terms then you will go a long way to getting the best out of your equipment. But, if not, then skip this chapter.

Receivers and transmitters

Before we go any further we must understand in simple terms just what receivers and transmitters are. The transmitter is a device which generates an electromagnetic signal that will radiate from an aerial. The power, that is, strength of the signal as it is transmitted is measured in watts. For instance, a CB radio transmitter may have a power of about four watts, but a medium wave broadcast transmitter power might be as much as 1 million watts — better known as a megawatt. The allowable transmitter power used in any application is normally stipulated in Government regulations. Obviously, a broadcast transmitter has to sends its signals long distances in order to reach the large number of people that make up the station's audience, so it will need to be of high power. On the other hand, a taxi firm operating in one town will only need to contact cabs over only a few miles and so the required power level is much lower. Normally, but there are exceptions, the transmitter sends out what is called a radio frequency 'carrier wave' and the speech, music or other information to be transmitted is superimposed on this wave. There are several 'modes' of doing this, discussed later in the chapter.

The receiver, in this case the scanner, needs an aerial to 'gather up' the radio frequency transmitted signal. The aerial is not selective enough to gather up the required signal alone, and a number of other signals that happen to be on the air at the same time are presented to the receiver. These signals are first 'amplified', that is, boosted, after which they enter a stage within the receiver where the wanted signal is isolated from the rest. This is further amplified before going through what is called a 'detector' or 'demodulator' which converts the radio frequency signal back into the speech, music or other information originally super-imposed on the carrier wave.

Most of the transmissions you hear on a scanner will be from equipment called 'transceivers' — the term is an abridged name for transmitter/receiver. That is because most scanners cover the radio bands allocated to communications therefore the stations you hear will be talking back and forth to each other and so will need to transmit *and* receive.

A scanner is a very sophisticated type of receiver. Instead of just being tuned to one frequency at a time, it has special circuits which allow a whole range of frequencies to be programmed in by the user. The scanner then steps through all these frequencies (usually referred to as channels), stopping when it finds a transmission. Once the transmission ends the scanner carries on through the channels to find the next one with a transmission taking place.

Frequency/wavelength spectrum

One of the first topics that causes confusion among newcomers to radio is that of the frequency spectrum and the corresponding relationship between frequency and wavelength. Having established that we are going to transmit a signal we have to transmit it at a particular frequency. At the receiving end, as you tune across the dial of a normal radio, you will find a whole range of transmissions, but each one is at a different point on the dial, that is, each has a different frequency. You are tuning through part of what is called the 'frequency spectrum'. In practical terms try and imagine a radio which does not have separate switched bands for, say, medium and long wave, but instead has a great big long tuning dial. Let's say that the left hand side is the lowest frequency for transmitting, corresponding to 15 kilohertz. That means that the received transmission at this point will 'resonate' or vibrate at 15 thousand cycles per second (kilo, in radio and electronics terms, simply means thousand: hertz means cycles per second). As we tune from left to right the received frequency becomes greater and we pass through those frequencies allocated for long wave broadcasting. When we get to about 550 kHz (kHz is the abbreviation for kilohertz) we come to the medium wave broadcast band which carries on up to 1600 kHz. However, at this point we drop the term kilohertz because 1600 kilohertz equals 1.6 megahertz (mega — meaning million). We carry on tuning upwards, passing through what is called medium frequency (MF for short) and we now come into what in the past has been referred to as short wave but is now known as high frequency (HF). We can continue tuning until we get even higher in frequency to 30 MHz (MHz is the abbreviation for megahertz). Above this we are in what is called very high frequency (VHF). We can carry on much further and will come next to ultra high frequency (UHF), then on to super high frequency (SHF) and extremely high frequency (EHF): more commonly called 'microwaves'.

Notice that all the time we have been talking about frequency we have related it to waves and wavelengths. That is because at any point on the dial we can define the transmission as a frequency *or* as a wavelength — any given frequency has a corresponding wavelength, and vice versa.

Table 2.1 relates the various frequency divisions together with the corresponding ranges. Dividing the radio frequency spectrum up in this

Table 2.1 Radio frequency spectrum, each division as a frequency range

Frequency division	Frequency range
Very low frequency (VLF)	3–30 kHz
Low frequency (LF)	30–300 kHz
Medium frequency (MF)	300–3000 kHz
High frequency (HF)	3–30 MHz
Very high frequency (VHF)	30–300 MHz
Ultra high frequency (UHF)	300–3000 MHz
Super high frequency (SHF)	3–30 GHz
Extremely high frequency (EHF)	30–300 GHz
No designation	300–3000 GHz

k = kilo = ×1,000
M = mega = ×1,000,000
G = giga = ×1,000,000,000

way is simply a matter of convenience — most radio transmitters and receivers aren't capable of tuning over the whole spectrum in one go, as our imaginary radio can, and switched divisions are required. The divisions given in Table 2.1 are those generally accepted worldwide.

From now on this book will be dealing mainly with the VHF and UHF division bands and so for the most part we will be talking about megahertz, although there will be reference to kilohertz when we discuss channel spacing and bandwidth.

So where do scanners fit in to all of this? Some, like the synthesised types, cover anywhere between 26 MHz at the top end of HF and, in the case of Icom, 2000 MHz (2 GHz) at UHF. There are also scanners which cover the HF bands, but they do not really cover the categories of communications dealt with by this book.

Distances

Now back to the question of distances we asked at the start of the chapter. In order to answer that question we need to look at what is called 'propagation', which is the way radio signals actually travel. There are three main ways a signal gets from one point to another:

As a **groundwave**. The signal travels virtually in a straight line between the two points.
As a **skywave**. The signal leaves one point, travels skywards and bounces off part of the ionosphere, back to earth.
Via **tropospherical ducting**. The signal travels above ground, through a conductive layer caused by the junction of warm and cold air currents.

Ground wave (Figure 2.1)
The ground wave is the main means of propagation for signals above 30 MHz. However, at frequencies slightly above and below 30 MHz, other conditions prevail at times but we will look at those in a moment.

Figure 2.1 Ground wave. Typically 'line of sight' at VHF and UHF.

For VHF and UHF communications it is generally fair to say that the ground wave transmission distance is limited to what is called 'line of sight'. That means that if there were no obstructions such as buildings or high ground around us the signal would only travel as far as we can see on a clear day, in other words to the horizon. In practical terms this means that communication between two stations on the ground is usually limited at the most to around 30 miles. Obviously if the transmitting station is on very high ground this range will increase and if we are flying at thousands of feet in an aircraft the range increases even further. Other factors which effect this range are such things as transmitter power; obviously the more powerful the transmitter the further the range, although there does come a point where even masses of increase in transmitter power will make little difference to the range of the signal.

Skywave (Figure 2.2)

As its name suggests, the skywave is that part of the signal from the transmitting aerial that travels upwards. Also known as ionospheric propagation, it is the main means of propagation of frequencies below 30 MHz. What happens is that the signal travels up to the ionosphere where it bounces back off one of the several layers of ionised gas. Normally the ionisation is not dense enough to bounce back the much smaller VHF and UHF radio waves. However it will bounce back the bigger waves encountered in the HF bands.

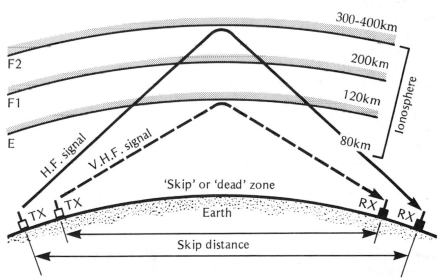

Figure 2.2 Sky wave. Note that VHF signals will not normally skip as far as HF signals.

We can draw an analogy here which will illustrate how this effect occurs: imagine the ionosphere as a screen of chicken mesh. If we gather a handful of different sized stones and think of the bigger stones as representing the lower HF frequencies while the smaller stones are the higher VHF/UHF frequencies; then throw our stones at the chicken mesh, the bigger stones bounce back at us but the smaller ones pass right through the mesh. In simple terms that is roughly what happens to our radio waves.

There are several different layers in the ionosphere which affect the skywave. They are the E, F1 and F2 layers. The F2 layer is the one largely responsible for bouncing back HF signals and at certain times (such as during the winter months and at night) it tends to combine with the F1 layer. The more densely ionised the gases are, the more they are capable of bouncing back signals at higher frequencies. The degree of ionisation depends on radiation from the sun and so during daylight hours and the summer months the ionisation increases and higher frequencies start bouncing back to earth. Put simply, the more ionisation, the higher in frequency the reflection occurs.

This phenomenon is also subject to quite spectacular peaks. There is an 11 year cycle in which solar flares on the sun's surface cause higher than usual radiation. In the lead up to this peak and after it, ionisation is so intense that it is not unusual for low powered signals to travel right round the world. This latter effect is called 'multi-hop' and here the signal hits the ionosphere, bounces back to earth, bounces back up again and so forth. The last peak of the cycle was in 1980

The area on the ground between the signal going up and coming back down again is known as the 'skip zone' or 'dead zone'. The distance a reflected signal travels between two points on the ground is called the 'skip distance'.

The skywave effect we have talked about so far is generally limited to frequencies below 50 MHz. Above that frequency, however, a similar effect takes place due to the E layer which reflects VHF signals. The phenomenon usually happens only during the summer months, when sudden heavy ionisation lasting but a very short period of time — just a few hours in some cases — occurs. Hence, the effect is known as 'sporadic-E'. It can affect frequencies from the upper end of HF to as high as 150 MHz in the VHF bands. Typical ranges under these conditions may be distances of 800 miles or more at VHF.

Above 150 MHz it becomes rarer for signals to be affected by any kind of reflection from the ionosphere.

Tropospherical ducting (Figure 2.3)
Tropospherical ducting is responsible for most of the freak long-distance reception that the scanner user will encounter.

The effect takes place at around 2000 metres above the ground, and occurs mostly during the summer when, under the right weather conditions, a cold air stream meets a warm air stream forming a sort of 'pipe' which ducts the signal along for great distances. Tropospherical ducting (so called because the 'pipe' is formed in the layer known as the

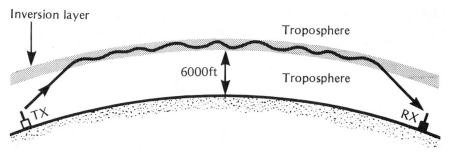

Figure 2.3 Tropospherical ducting 'Tropo'.

troposphere) is most common at VHF and UHF frequencies, but it can extend to microwaves at times.

Ranges under these conditions vary enormously but, as an example, it is quite common to work distances of several hundred miles or more in the 2 metre amateur band.

Any effect, such as these three, which occurs to increase the range of the signals is often referred to as a 'lift' or 'lift conditions'.

Modes of modulation (Figure 2.4)

The simplest of radio signals consist of nothing more than a carrier wave switched on and off. If the switching is spaced to produce dots and dashes we have morse code, or CW as it is often called. The average

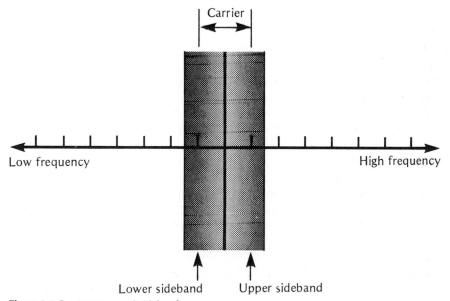

Figure 2.4 Carrier wave and sidebands.

scanner user is unlikely to be interested in morse code and, indeed, the majority of scanners are not capable of reproducing it anyway.

What is of more interest is a carrier wave that has an audio signal such as speech superimposed on it. There are several ways of superimposing an audio signal on a radio carrier wave signal and one method even does away with the carrier wave altogether.

Amplitude modulation (AM)

In amplitude modulation the audio signal is used to control the amplitude of the carrier. If we display this graphically on an oscilloscope we see that, in fact, the carrier is broken up into what are known as 'envelopes' (see Figure 2.5). The envelopes change in sympathy with the

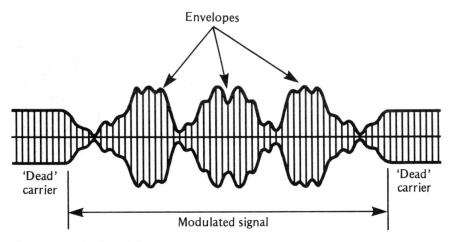

Figure 2.5 Amplitude modulation.

audio signal. At the receiving end the simple circuit that converts the amplitude modulated carrier back into an audio signal is called a 'detector'. Unfortunately its simplicity can cause problems for other electronic equipment sited near the transmitter. One problem is the breakthrough of signals into equipment such as record players, baby alarms, intercoms, etc, containing audio amplifiers. The solid state devices in these amplifiers can, given a strong enough signal, act as detectors which reproduce the transmitted signal.

AM as a mode is now largely being superseded by FM which has several advantages, one of which is that it does not cause the same level of breakthrough. AM is still in use, though, on some private mobile radio bands, some European CB channels and the international aircraft band.

Frequency modulation (FM)

This works on an entirely different concept, illustrated in Figure 2.6. Here the *frequency* of the carrier is shifted rapidly up and down in sympathy with the audio signal. The difference in frequency between the lowest and highest points is called the 'deviation'. In a broadcast FM transmitter the deviation may be as much as 150 kHz but, in the case of a transceiver which a scanner tunes into, deviation is kept quite low to limit its use of the radio spectrum (typically 5 kHz).

The smaller the deviation, the smaller is the transmitted radio signal 'bandwidth', ie, the amount of frequency spectrum taken up by the radio signal. A small, or narrow bandwidth means that the signal will take up less space in a given band and for communication bands this means we are able to slot more channels into a given band. The result obviously is that we can get more users on the air in a given band space.

At the receiving end, the method of converting the signal back into audio is far more complex than with AM. The circuit that does the

Constant amplitude

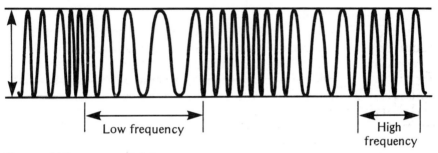

Figure 2.6(a) Frequency modulation.

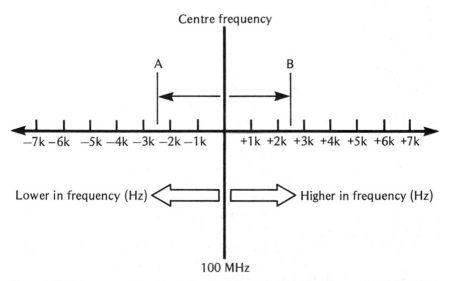

Figure 2.6(b) How a narrowband (speech only) FM signal would look if we could graphically show it on a radio dial. The lowest frequency (bass) sounds would shift the frequency towards 'A' whilst the highest sounds (treble) would shift towards 'B'.

conversion is known as a 'demodulator' or 'discriminator'. It is the complexity of this conversion process that makes the mode less likely to be demodulated by circuitry in audio equipment of the type that AM can interfere with.

FM is now widely used in communications. It will be found on most land mobile allocations and is the only mode used on the marine VHF band.

An AM detector *can* be used to resolve an FM signal just as an FM detector *can* resolve an AM signal. However, in both instances the received audio will be noisy, weak and probably distorted. Wherever possible the correct demodulator/detector should be used. It is possible to get passable reception of an FM signal from an AM detector by slightly off-tuning. The receiver is then partly tuned into the side-band and this method of operation is known as 'slope detection'.

Single sideband (SSB)

Refer back to Figure 2.4 and you will see that we still have not talked about the two sidebands. Each sideband actually contains all the information relating to the transmitted audio signal, so in theory it is possible to transmit the signal without a carrier at all. Nevertheless, the audio signal is initially superimposed onto the carrier in a similar way to AM transmission.

However, special filters in the transmitter remove the carrier wave and one of the sidebands. Most SSB transmitters have a switch that allows either the upper or lower sideband to be removed. With only a single sideband to be transmitted it is apparent that even less bandspace than either AM or FM is required so a greater number of channels may be crammed into a given band.

SSB may seem the ideal solution to the crowded airwaves but unfortunately it has some drawbacks — particularly for mobile operation. At the receiving end we have to re-insert the missing carrier wave before we can carry out the detection process. The carrier wave we put back in is generated by a beat frequency oscillator (BFO) which has to be tuned precisely to match the frequency of the incoming signal . . . even the slightest off-tuning can make the detected audio signal distorted, sounding very much like someone imitating Donald Duck. Obviously, a mobile operator cannot drive and re-tune at the same time. A further problem exists because the circuits in the transmitter and receiver are far more complex than AM or FM equivalents, so SSB equipment is far more costly.

The greatest users of SSB on the VHF/UHF bands are amateurs and in Chapter 7 you will find bandplans for the amateur service which show where most SSB operation takes place. However, there are only two scanners available in the UK that can properly receive SSB transmissions. These are the Yaesu and Icom.

For the practically adept, a suitable circuit to modify the SX-200 is available in kit form from Cirkit (address at back of book). Having fitted one of these to my own SX-200 I can see no reason why it should not be adapted to other sets although a suitable injection point for the BFO signal is required.

The fine tuning needed for SSB is carried out in one of two ways. On better equipment, the switch marked USB (upper sideband) or LSB (lower sideband) will switch the BFO to the appropriate frequency. Fine tuning of the receiver is then carried out until clear speech is heard.

The second method, found on cheaper equipment, is a bit cruder. First, the receiver is tuned roughly to the incoming signal; second, the BFO frequency is tuned to get clear speech. The disadvantage with this method is that it is often necessary to jiggle around between the receiver's tuning and BFO setting to get it right.

Channelising (Figure 2.7)

Channelising is often something of a mystery to the newcomer to radio and yet it is quite simple to understand.

We can take part of the radio spectrum and divide it up into blocks. If, for instance, we were to take that segment of the spectrum from 150 to 150.90 MHz we could divide it up into 10 'spot frequencies' starting with 150.00 MHz, then 150.10 MHz, then 150.20 MHz and so forth until we

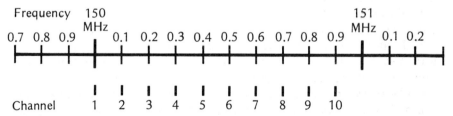

Figure 2.7 Channelising. Any section of the radio spectrum can be divided up and each spot frequency given a channel number.

reach 150.90 MHz. We now have 10 spot frequencies, with separations of 100 KHz, which may be allocated as radio transmission channels and could be numbered, in this case, from 1 to 10. We can do this to any part of the radio spectrum although, in practice, it does not always follow that the channels are numbered in the sequence they appear in the spectrum. Take a look at the Marine bands in Chapter 7 and you will see a typical example of this.

A large proportion of the VHF/UHF spectrum is split up into channels. In some bands, they are referred to by a channel number but in other bands by the actual frequency that the channel is on. Again, you will see in Chapter 7 that the entire marine band is referred to by channel numbers. However, although the aircraft band is also divided up into channels, they are always referred to by frequency.

The separation between channels quite naturally is referred to as 'channel separation'. This separation tends to vary a bit between the different bands simply because over the years some separations have been reduced to fit more channels into a given band. Typical these days, though, is 12.5 kHz separation at VHF and 25 kHz separation at UHF. Remember what we said earlier about limiting the deviation to around 5 kHz at VHF. If we deduct that from the 12.5 kHz separation we get 7.5 kHz. Divide that by two to get 3.75 kHz and that is the amount of spare space either side of the transmitted signal. This space, sometimes called a 'guard band', ensures that the signal does not splash over into the next channel causing interference to other operators.

As a general rule, any band where the operator is permitted to use a range of frequencies will be split up into numbered channels. It is easier and quicker for, say, CB or marine operators, to say to each other 'change to channel 10' than it is to start rattling off an actual frequency — allowing they could remember what the centre frequency of a particular channel is.

On the other hand, private mobile radio operators who work solely on their own allocated channel will have it allocated as a frequency. So, the PMR bands *are* split up into channels, however, they are not numbered and are referred to by frequency.

Types of transmission

The VHF/UHF bands are used for a variety of transmissions and these fall into four broad categories; audio, morse, television and data (teletype, fax, etc). These categories must not be confused with modulation modes. Most of the following transmission types can be transmitted in any mode.

Audio
This, of course, takes the form of simple speech or, in the case of broadcasts, it may be music. Indeed any sounds that the human ear can interpret may be transmitted.

Morse
One of the simplest forms of communications, morse consists of nothing more than a series of dots and dashes. The duration of the switching on and off of a carrier wave makes up the dots and dashes which can be interpreted by a skilled operator into letters, numbers and punctuation.

Although there *are* morse transmissions at VHF/UHF, few scanners are able to receive them. The transmitted signal contains no tone of any kind and, in order to get the familiar 'beep', the scanner must be fitted with a beat frequency oscillator. Without this, morse will simply sound like a series of soft rhythmic clicks.

Television

This can take two forms. The most familiar types are normal broadcast transmissions which are known as 'broadband/fast scan'. The Yaesu-Musen is one of the few scanners that has the circuitry (as an optional extra) to demodulate television signals. However, this facility is of little use to European users as the output format is the American NTSC and is not compatible with European systems such as PAL.

Amateurs also use this type of transmission to send not only black and white but also colour pictures between themselves. Special equipment is needed for this and operation is limited to the UHF bands.

Another form of television used by amateurs is called 'slow scan television'; SSTV for short. This is a method of sending drawings and still photographs, taking several seconds to transmit a single frame, which is built up slowly, line by line. Scanner owners who are interested in these transmissions will be interested to know that if they also own one of the popular home micro-computers, then using a simple adaptor and appropriate software it is possible to reproduce these pictures on a normal television set. Details of adaptors and software are given in Chapter 6.

If, when scanning amateur bands, you hear what sounds like a period of buzzing noises that rise and fall in pitch with a regular blip at the end of each burst, then it is probably SSTV.

Facsimile

This again is a method of sending drawings or still pictures over the air. Popularly called 'fax', it works on virtually identical principles to SSTV. Scanner users can easily pick-up fax transmissions from the weather satellites and, as with SSTV, it is possible to convert these signals (which usually sound like a series of bleeps or tones) with the help of a home computer. Again Chapter 6 gives more details.

RTTY

RTTY (an acronym for radio teletype) is, simply, a teleprinter used to send messages by radio rather than by telephone line. RTTY is used at VHF/UHF by amateurs and, again, it is a means of communication that can be decoded by a home computer. However, to receive these transmissons you will need to have a BFO circuit on the receiver (see the morse code section above). The received signals sound like speeded up morse code although they do actually consist of two alternating tones.

ASCII

ASCII (the American Standard Code for Information Interchange) is the 'language' that computers use to store and send programs or data, and it is occasionally transmitted, particularly by amateurs when they want to swap computer programs, over the air. Although many scanners are capable of receiving such transmissions, which sound exactly like a computer program cassette played back through a loudspeaker, any transmissions received will only be of use if the scanner owner owns a compatible computer. However, such transmissions are usually preceded by normal voice communications between the amateurs concerned and so some idea will be gained of what the program is, which computer it is for and when they are going to start sending. Should the scanner owner be able to make use of the program then it is simply a matter of recording it off air via the scanner's record or earphone socket.

Odd sounds

Occasionally odd signals may be heard which do not fit into any of the above categories. These can be anything from navigation beacons to telemetry signals sending data.

Simplex/Duplex operation

There is often misunderstanding over the expressions 'simplex' and 'duplex', together with their derivatives, and the situation is not helped by the fact that different groups of communications users have different interpretations. Generally, the terms refer to whether the communication is one-way at a time, or two-way. For the purposes of this book, the following definitions are assumed.

Simplex

This is the easiest operation to understand. For instance you will hear typical simplex transmissons on the civilian aircraft band. You can hear both sides of a conversation on one frequency. So we know that station A transmits on a particular frequency, while station B listens. Then station B transmits on the same frequency while station A listens. In other words only one station transmits at any one time, and only one frequency is used, so one station must wait for the other to finish transmission, before transmitting itself.

Split or dual frequency simplex (Figure 2.8)

In some sections of the VHF/UHF spectrum, you may well pick up transmissions where you can only hear one side of a conversation, even though the station you cannot hear may be in range. There are several types of this kind of communications which use two frequencies instead

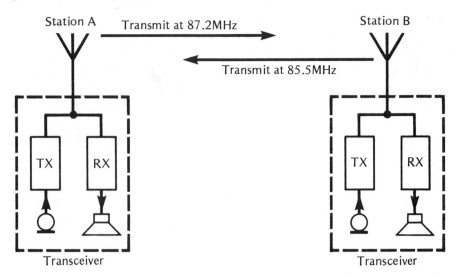

Transmitter frequency: 87.2MHz
Receiver frequency: 85.5MHz

Transmitter frequency: 85.5MHz
Receiver frequency: 87.2MHz

Figure 2.8 Split frequency simplex.

of one and the example we consider here is known as 'split frequency simplex'. In this, station A transmits on, say, 85.5 MHz. But when station B transmits, a different frequency, say, 87.2 MHz, is used. Each station still must wait its turn to transmit. When picking up these kinds of transmission the scanner owner has to programme both frequencies into his scanner in order to hear both sides of the conversation.

It may well seem that it is a waste of spectrum space to use two frequencies for communications when ordinary simplex could have been used to achieve the same end result. However, split frequency simplex has some advantages for some communicators, the greatest of which is that it allows the use of what are known as 'repeaters' (see Figure 2.9). Let us assume that the repeater and its aerials (one for receive the other for transmit) are on good high ground. Portable set A transmits and is picked up by the base station receiver which feeds the signal to the base station transmitter and re-broadcasts it. Portable set b, which is well out of normal working distance from portable A is able to pick up the signals easily. And of course the system will work in reverse allowing B to talk back to A.

Repeaters, as used by amateurs, operate like this all the time. They have computer controlled circuitry to switch the transmitter on when a signal is received and shut down again when no one is using it. Some repeaters activate automatically on any signal containing speech others require a short burst of tone from the incoming signal to switch on. Repeaters are not supposed to be used for long conversations and so

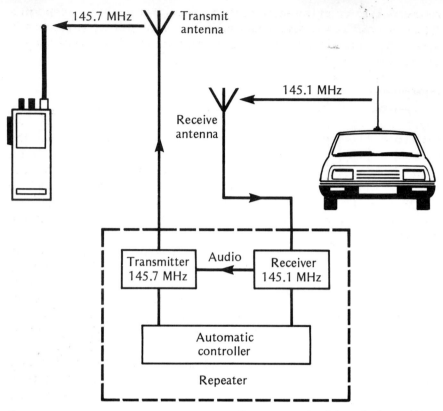

Figure 2.9 Repeater. Automatic turn-on and turn-off. In the case of 'talkthrough' the switching controller is operated manually.

have a built-in timer which switches the transmitter off after a pre-determined time.

Another advantage of split frequency simplex is that it allows 'talkthrough'. Talkthrough is often used by such bodies as the police for the odd occasion that two mobile units may need to liaise with each other. In this case the talkthrough is actually switched over manually at the base station or control centre.

Although these are instances of split frequency working, the scanner needs only be tuned to the output of the repeater to be able to hear both sides of the conversation.

Duplex

Duplex operation is most easily understood with reference to the telephone, where two-way communications can take place simultaneously, that is, both users can speak and listen at the same time. A dual frequency method of working as described in split frequency simplex is used, but here the stations have their transmitters and receivers both on at the same time. It means that a normal telephone-type conversation can take place and indeed duplex operation is mostly used to put normal telephone calls, over the air, to ships, cars and in the case of the USA, aircraft.

Half duplex

This works in a similar way to duplex operation but is not quite so sophisticated, even though it does allow a radio system to be connected to the normal telephone system. The base station operates in much the same way as in duplex in that the transmitter and receiver will both be on at the same time. However, the mobile unit is only able to transmit *or* receive at any one time. In some instances, the operator needs to key the microphone but in other cases a circuit called a 'vox', short for voice operated switch, will automatically switch to transmit every time the mobile operator speaks.

Scanner users are most likely to encounter half duplex operation on the marine bands and mobile telephone frequencies. On the marine bands it is used for a system known as 'link calls', where communications between ship and shore allow telephone calls to be either originated or received on the vessel. Similarly, the system is used extensively for mobile telephones in cars on networks available in some larger cities.

Both duplex and half duplex operations present some problems for the scanner owner because, as two frequencies are being used simultaneously, it is only possible to pick up one side of the conversation.

3 The hardware

Scanners come in a variety of shapes, sizes and types. They also vary very much in quality and performance. As a general rule, though, they are more sophisticated and built to a higher standard than most portable radios used for broadcast reception. They are designed to cover a number of frequencies so that they may be used to monitor several transmissions. This, of course, is because communications signals, unlike broadcasts, are not transmitted constantly and are only transmitted when there are messages.

In order to fully cover the different types of scanner we have to divide them into two distinct types; 'crystal controlled' and synthesised. In the case of crystal controlled scanners it is necessary to plug into the circuit small quartz crystals which oscillate at the frequency you want to receive. Once you have installed such a crystal you are stuck with that frequency — other crystals are needed for different frequencies.

Synthesised scanners, on the other hand, don't need such crystals. They incorporate a sophisticated circuit, which is controlled by a small computer, to generate the frequencies required. Any change in frequency is merely programmed in, usually through a calculator-style keyboard on the front panel.

As a rule, crystal controlled scanners are much cheaper than synthesised ones but bear in mind that crystals are expensive. In the case of, say, a ten channel air band scanner, the ten crystals might cost as much as the scanner itself.

Crystal controlled scanners

The photo on page 145 shows a typical crystal controlled scanner. These were the first scanners ever to appear and, despite their main disadvantage of crystal changing requirements, are still popular. They are normally only capable of covering a small number of channels: a minimum of about four and a maximum of about 16. Also, these channels must be fairly close together in frequency. However, there is an exception in some of the models sold by the Tandy Corporation, which are capable of tuning over two given bands, with a certain number of channels allocated to each of those bands.

The main advantage of crystal controlled scanners is that they can be made quite small — there are examples of units covering as many as ten channels while still being little bigger than the size of a cigarette packet.

Chapter 4 gives details on how to change the crystals in these scanners.

Synthesised scanners

The photo on page 136 shows a typical synthesised scanner. Synthesised scanners sub-divide into two categories. The first works in a similar way to the crystal controlled types but the difference is that a synthesiser is used for tuning instead. Such scanners allow you to programme in a number of channels but do not allow instant access from front panel controls to dial in new channels. So like crystal controlled scanners, although no expensive crystals are involved, the scanner is limited to stepping through pre-set channels.

A variation on this method is 'frequency-stepping' via buttons on the front panel. This type of programming is found on such sets as the 'Fairmate' and 'Signal R-532'. Here there are several buttons, one steps in units of 10 MHz, the next in 1 MHz, then 100 KHz, and so on. The procedure is to keep pressing the buttons until the required digits appear on the digital frequency readout. The method is a bit like the system used to set digital timers and clocks on such things as videorecorders. This type of programming presents no problems where only a selection of pre-set channels are ever monitored. However, it is a very slow method of programming and not suited to rapid entry of a new frequency. Sets with calculator-type input keyboards are much quicker.

The second kind of synthesised scanner offers the same programmed-channel scan facility as the previous type of synthesised scanner but can also 'search' for signals by continuously and automatically tuning through the bands. For instance, you can programme the scanner to search from, say, 100 MHz to 200 MHz, whereupon it will start at the lowest frequency and slowly tune upwards to the highest. If it finds any transmissions it will lock onto them but, if not, it will start again at the bottom and again work through the selected band. The big advantage this offers is that it enables the user to find all sorts of transmissions previously unheard. Once found, a communication channel frequency may be programmed into the scanner's memory, for use another time.

Another big advantage with this facility is that it's possible to locate a particular transmission when only an approximate frequency is known.

For instance if you knew a certain station occasionally transmitted at about 145.5 MHz you can set the scanner to search rapidly over and over again between 145 and 146 MHz until the station starts to transmit.

In addition to searching you can of course use these sets for true scanning. That is getting the equipment to run through a series of channels that you have programmed with the frequencies you want to listen in to. Most current sets have memories for 16 or more channels which hold the channel frequencies even when the set is switched off. A couple of small cells or a special capacitor provide power requirements for the memory circuit. Normally the batteries will last a year or more but users should always remember to write down the frequencies because when the batteries require replacement all channels will require consequent re-programming. In the case of scanners such as the AOR, a small capacitor holds enough charge to keep the memory active. Although the capacitor is re-charged every time the set is used it is only good for about a fortnight between charges.

Frequency coverage

Scanners vary enormously in the range of frequencies that they cover. More modern and expensive ones like the AOR2002, SX-400, Yaesu-Musen and Icom cover a very wide range of frequencies from VHF through to UHF. Other sets, though, such as most of the Bearcats and Radio-Shack (Tandy) models and the SX-200 leave out certain frequency bands and so there are gaps in their coverage. At times this can be a nuisance because it means you cannot tune-in to certain interesting bands. The reason some scanners skip certain bands is because it is either cheaper for them to be made that way or they are not really designed for the European markets. Most scanners are made in Japan and are designed for the American market. In the USA some bands are allocated for entirely different kinds of transmissions to those used in Europe. As an example, owners of the SX-200 have often been frustrated that the set does not cover the section of the VHF band from 88 to 108 MHz. In America this band is used exclusively for VHF broadcasting which is of little interest to scanner users, but in Britain it is presently used for such things as private mobile radio and emergency service transmissions, too.

When choosing a scanner it is a good idea to have a list of the frequencies you wish to cover before deciding on the model you will buy. It is not unknown for salesmen, often through sheer ignorance, to completely misinform a potential customer on what transmissions a particular type of scanner will pick up. Details of who transmits on what frequencies are covered in Chapter 7.

Strange switches and knobs

For the newcomer to scanning, the front panel of his equipment can present a bewildering array of control knobs and switches often labelled with unfamiliar names (see Photo 3(a). Unlike the elaborate knobs and switches found on some modern hi-fi equipment these controls are not just for show. The wide range of conditions found on communications frequencies means the scanner owner must be able to select various options for such things as mode, channel spacing, bandwidth, etc.

Photograph 3(a) A typical modern scanner control panel. Note that several of the push-buttons double up for more than one use such as mode or step rate as well as a digit for frequency entry.

Usually, the more expensive the scanner the more control the owner has over the way it operates. There follows descriptions of most controls found on modern scanners.

Squelch or mute

A 'squelch' control, occasionally called 'mute', can be found on most types of VHF and UHF equipment used in communications. It is a form of electronic switch which cuts off the audio signal when the radio is not receiving anything. The reason for this is quite simple: if the scanner is tuned to a channel with no transmission in it and the audio was not switched off, the listener would have to put up with the constant roaring hiss of amplifying circuits, the crackle of static and noise from a variety of sources of interference. In scanning, the control takes on another important role because the circuit that actually steps through the pre-programmed channels is activated by the squelch. So when there is no received signal the squelch tells the scanner to keep hunting until it finds a channel where there is someone transmitting. Once found the squelch 'opens' and that causes the scanning circuit to stop and so lock on to that active channel.

There are three main types of squelch found on scanners. Some sets will only include one type whereas more elaborate equipment will allow the operator to select the kind of squelch he wishes to use.

Carrier squelch

This is the simplest (in electrical terms) kind of squelch and is best situated to reception of AM signals. It works by detecting the presence of a carrier wave and simply shuts the audio on and off. The main disadvantage of this type of squelch is that it will activate on some types of interference such as car ignition noise and static.

Deviation muting

Despite the term muting, it is still squelch and in this instance is only suitable for FM reception. However, it is far more effective than carrier squelch when it comes to ignoring the types of interference mentioned above. This type of squelch is often encountered as the sole means of muting on some crystal controlled scanners such as the pocket-sized ones available for the amateur 2 metre and and marine bands. This type of squelch does not respond to varying signal strength but instead detects the actual deviation (see Chapter 2) of the FM signal.

Voice squelch

Also known as 'AF scan', voice squelch is a fairly specialised form of squelch, usually found on more expensive sets. It works in a very different way to carrier and deviation muting, in which the actual triggering takes place when any incoming signal is detected. Voice squelch needs not only an incoming signal but also speech or other form of modulation. This means it will not respond to a plain carrier signal. One of the main uses for this kind of squelch is to avoid locking onto oscillations generated within the scanner itself, known as 'birdies'. They appear to the scanner as a carrier wave and the simplest way to check for their presence is to unplug the aerial. If a 'carrier wave' is still present then it is a birdie. They can be a nuisance when searching between frequencies but with voice squelch, the scanner will ignore them. One tip, when listening to simplex transmissions, is to also insert 'delay' (see the following control) otherwise the scanner will carry on searching even when it has found a transmission.

Squelch delay

This is a feature only found on more expensive scanners and it allows the user to get the scanner to wait for a few seconds at the end of a transmission. Normally, once a station has sent its message, the transmission ceases and the scanner starts searching again. This can be a nuisance in some circumstances. Say, for instance, you are trying to listen to a conversation between two stations but each time one of them stops transmitting to let the other station reply, your scanner zooms off through the rest of its channels. At best you have to wait for the scanner to come back to the channel, by which time you will have missed part of the conversation and at worst you will miss everything else because your scanner locks onto a transmission on another channel.

With squelch delay it is possible to get the scanning circuit to wait for a few seconds, to see if there is going to be another transmission, before starting to scan other channels.

Obviously this facility is only needed with single frequency simplex transmission (amateur, aircraft, some marine channels, etc). There, both stations are on the same frequency or channel. Squelch delay is not required with split frequency simplex: in that case you would want the scanner to get as quickly as possible to the other channel where the second station will transmit its reply.

On some scanners it is possible to program the delay facility into memory along with the channel frequency so that delay occurs only on required channels.

Pre-set squelch

While most scanners allow the user to adjust the point at which the squelch opens and closes, some smaller sets such as pocket portables have a pre-set squelch control. This usually takes the form of a small trimming component on the circuit board rather than the rotary or slider resistor type provided as a front panel control. Be warned, though, that it is not a good idea to go delving inside your scanner to adjust this control unless you know what you are doing. Failure to ignore this warning could be expensive and your scanner would not be the first to arrive back at a service workshop in need of complete re-alignment because the wrong trimmers have been 'tweaked'.

Squelch override, squelch defeat, mute defeat

Featured on scanners with pre-set squelch, a push button which manually opens the squelch circuit. Useful if the signal is very weak or varying in reception strength.

Using squelch

The normal variable squelch found on most scanners must be used properly. On turning the squelch control gently there will come a point where the background noise suddenly disappears — this is the ideal squelch setting. If the control is turned further stronger and stronger signals are required to open the squelch circuit. Some of the channels stored in memory will have a higher background noise than others, so if the squelch keeps opening on a dead channel merely increase the setting slightly, to compensate, allowing the scanner to step through the complete scanning range. However, never set the squelch any higher than you have to. Winding it to full will almost certainly block out all but the very strongest of signals.

Some squelch circuits have 'hysteresis'. This means there is a slight difference in sensitivity between their 'on' and 'off' points. It becomes noticeable when the scanner stops on a signal but the squelch does not close again when the signal disappears. Again it is simply a question of advancing the control slightly to overcome the effect.

Automatic noise limiter (ANL)
A switch which minimises the effects of pulse-type interference, such as the interference caused by ignition circuits in cars.

Automatic frequency control (AFC)
This circuit is rarely encountered on scanners but is sometimes found on special monitor receivers. It is a circuit that will automatically track slight changes in frequency by the transmitting station. It is particularly useful on receivers designed for satellite reception. Orbiting satellites travel at high speed and signal reception may be therefore subject to what is known as 'Doppler shift' — an apparent change in received frequency AFC will track the tuning for these slight changes.

Auto-write scan
Allows the scanner to search all channels between two pre-set frequencies (normal search) and if it comes across any transmission the frequency of the channel is memorised.

Bandwidth
You will recall that earlier in the book (Chapter 2) we explained that different kinds of transmission take up different bandwidths, eg, communications transmissions are quite narrow while broadcast transmissions are relatively wide. Most scanners are designed to receive narrow bandwidth channels although in some cases they may switch automatically to slightly wider bandwidths at UHF. This is because UHF channels are spaced slightly further apart than VHF ones. Some of the newer scanners on the market do offer the option of switching to the kind of wide bandwidth needed to listen to broadcast transmissions and

some sets even go as far as allowing the required bandwidth to be programmed for each individual channel stored in the memory.

Selector buttons are usually marked NFM, NAM (or just AM) and WFM, where N stands for 'narrow' and W stands for 'wide'.

Clear (M-clear)

This switch clears all data such as frequency, mode, etc, in memory, so freeing the memory and allowing the user to program new data in.

Dial

On some scanners this tranfers control from the automatic up/down search to the manual tuning control knob.

Dial to memory (D ▷ M)

On scanners with a manual tuning control this allows a frequency that has been manually tuned-in to be entered into memory at the press of a button.

Down (▽)

Instructs the scanner to search downwards in frequency. See also 'UP' control.

Enter

Instructs the scanner to put information into memory.

Fine tune

Many synthesised scanners have a small fine tuning control which allows tuning slightly to either side of the centre frequency of the channel — useful when a transmitter is sending a signal slightly off-frequency from normal. Occasionally, it can be used to receive an FM signal while the scanner is in AM mode. By tuning to the side of the FM signal we tune slightly into the side-band allowing the scanner to resolve the signal by a 'slope detection' method.

Full tuning

This feature has only recently appeared on some sets and is an addition to the more familar search mode. An example of this facility is seen on the Yaesu-Musen scanner and it looks like a normal tuning knob. In fact it is a clever rotary switch which allows the user to manually tune up or down, allowing the user to search around channels at his own pace rather than at the normal search stepping speed. Many people still prefer the feel of a conventional tuning knob and this facility does provide it. A nice extra if you can afford a set with it on (Yaesu, AOR2002, Icom).

Key lock
Disables the keyboard so that settings cannot be accidentally disturbed.

Lock-out
There may be times when the scanner owner wants to listen to only a few of the channels that he has programmed into memory. In cases like this it is possible on some scanners to miss out those channels that are not required. This is accomplished by using 'lock-out'. The method employed varies with different scanners but usually takes one of two forms. On simple crystal controlled scanners each channel may simply have a switch which brings that channel into the scan or leaves it out. On synthesised scanners the principle is similar but usually done by a keyboard command rather than individual switches.

The second variation is where the scanner has two scanning sequences. One includes all the channels in the memory but the other includes only certain channels that are selected by the keyboard. This second search pattern, often called 'search B', can include as few or as many memory channels as required.

Manual
Allows the user to stop the scanner and use it instead to monitor a channel not in memory. On some sets the 'manual' control also tells the scanner to get ready to memorise a new channel frequency.

Memory count
Available on the Bearcat 250, it counts the number of times the scanner stops on a particular channel. The number can be recalled and so provide a useful guide as to which channels are the most 'active' in an area.

Memory to dial (M ▷ D)
This allows a channel frequency in memory to be recalled at the press of a button and for manual tuning to then be available to tune up or down from that frequency. Useful, for example, if the scanner is tuned to a channel in one band and the user wishes to re-tune to another band — simply pressing the button associated with a channel in the desired band does the job.

Mode selector

Some scanners will only operate in one mode. For instance 2 metre amateur and marine band scanners only receive FM while scanners designed solely for the aircraft band only receive AM. Even some synthesised scanners such as those in the Bearcat range do not allow the user to select the mode even though they cover both AM and FM channels: the circuit automatically switches to AM or FM depending on which band the scanned channel is in. Some scanners allow the user to choose between AM or FM, but do not allow reception of AM *and* FM channels in one scan. A typical example is the SX-200 which has a simple AM/FM switch on the front panel. The disadvantage here is that the scanner cannot properly receive, say, both marine (FM) *and* aircraft (AM) bands together in one scan.

However, some scanners (the SX-400 and AORs, Yaesu and Icom are typical examples) allow the user to program each memory channel not only with the channel frequency but also the mode.

Priority channel (PRI, PRIO)

This feature allows one channel to be programmed as a prime or priority channel. In other words, during the scan sequence, the priority channel is scanned more times than the others. A typical scan sequence on such receivers would be: scan channel 1 — scan priority — scan 2 — scan priority — scan 3, etc. An example of the use of this facility is when scanning the marine band where channel 16 (which is the calling and distress channel) could be scanned more than the others. Some scanners allow the user to decide which channel will have priority, whereas others, such as the AORs, always assume channel 1 as the priority channel.

Readouts, dials and lights

Simple crystal controlled scanners rarely incorporate anything more elaborate than a small LED lamp for each channel to show which one is actually being received when scanning stops. However synthesised scanners usually have some means of providing more information. A typical type of readout is a digital one showing not only the received frequency but also the number of the memory channel into which it is programmed. Obviously frequency readout is very important where a scanner with search facilities is concerned as without it it would be impossible to ever know where to look again for any station that you came across.

A scanner's digital readout of frequency is very accurate and some users rely on them as measuring instruments, for checking the frequency of transmitting equipment.

RF attenuator (ATT)

Also sometimes marked as a local/dx switch, this allows the scanner to be desensitised. The main use of this switch is to stop strong signals from nearby transmitters from causing interference.

Scan rate

This is a control which allows the speed at which the scanner steps through the scan sequence to be changed.

Search stop

Found on the Bearcat 250: the scanner searches until a transmission is received, but does not resume searching when the transmission stops. This allows the user time to check the frequency and put it into memory.

Signal meter (S meter)

A facility only found on more expensive sets which measures the strength of the incoming signal. It can be used in conjunction with fine tuning controls to ensure that the transmission is accurately tuned and is also a good way of checking on what conditions are like due to such things as the weather by keeping a check on the signal strength of, say, a known distant beacon transmitter. It can also be used for checking out the effectiveness of different kinds of aerial by comparing the received signal strengths from a reference source such as a beacon.

There are two main types of signal meter; a bargraph type consisting of a row of LED lights or a conventional moving coil meter with a pointer.

Step

Found on simple crystal controlled scanners, this is a push button that allows the channels in memory to be stepped through manually. Useful to stop the scan and set the receiver to stay on one particular channel.

Step rate (search rate)

Some scanners allow a degree of control over their stepping rate in the search mode. If you imagine the search facility as a sort of tuning knob that is automatically being turned for you then you get a rough idea of how search works. However, unlike a conventional tuning control which is fully variable, a scanner's search facility moves up or down in small steps. Typical steps are 12.5 kilohertz per step at VHF and 25 kilohertz per step at UHF. Most synthesised scanners set these rates automatically for whichever band they are scanning, as they are typical of the channel spacing for those bands. However, some more expensive sets allow you to set your own stepping rate. For scanners capable of receiving SSB transmissions this is vital because of the tuning accuracy required — these scanners need to have stepping rates as low as 100 hertz.

Up (△)

In search mode this tells the scanner to tune upwards in frequency. Like the DOWN (▽) control it is a search command.

Inputs and outputs

All scanners need connections for incoming and outgoing signals. For instance, we have to get radio signals in and so need a socket for the aerial. Next, having plugged an aerial to the scanner, we may well be content to listen to received transmissions on the built-in loudspeaker. However, even the simplest of scanners usually offers at least some kind of socket for either an external loudspeaker or earpiece.

Audio outputs

The quality of loudspeakers built into most scanners is usually defined as a compromise between cost and space saving. Even pocket-sized scanners can be improved on, when used at home, by plugging them into a bigger external speaker. Bigger scanners will also benefit from being run into a good quality loudspeaker which will give far clearer audio.

Another form of audio output found on some sets is the 'record' socket. This provides a low-level output (not amplified enough to feed a loudspeaker) which can be fed either to a tape recorder or separate amplifier. That secondary use can be useful in noisy environments where the scanner's internal amplifier is not powerful enough to provide enough volume. For instance, the early version of the SX-200 (prior to the 200N series) had an output that could barely be heard in a noisy vehicle. Several owners used a small separate amplifier giving a few watts output to solve the problem.

This socket can obviously also be used for recording transmissions (remember the warning at the front of the book though) and its output usually remains at a constant level which is not affected by the setting of the scanner's volume control.

Switching control

This is a refinement found on some expensive scanners. It is an electronic switch which is coupled to the squelch and switches on when a signal is present. It is used mostly to turn a tape recorder on and off so that transmissions during scanning can be recorded without wasting tape. A useful facility, but be warned that sets such as the SX-200 have such a connection but still need a small external control circuit to do the switching ... in other words you cannot just plug your recorder's remote control plug into the scanner.

Computer control

This is an input/output socket, usually configured as a serial interface, which allows a scanner to be controlled externally by a home computer. It is a facility found on only the most expensive scanners and the adaptor to connect to the computer is an optional extra. Connection is usually via the home computer's V24 (sometimes called: RS232C) port. With such a system, massively increased control over the scanner's functions is possible using relatively simple software. For instance, it becomes possible to increase the number of memories available, as well as adding sophisticated controlling sequences. In some cases it is possible to devote a memory 'page' in the computer to hold channel frequency, mode and bandwidth details as well as store user's notes about the channel.

The point about computer control is that all scanner functions become controllable by the user, via a computer keyboard and controlling programs. The user is no longer limited by the functions, features and sequences which the manufacturer builds into the scanner, but can now define his own. Computer control is one of the biggest steps forward in scanner technology over recent years.

IF output

This is a connection socket usually found on scanners, such as the SX-400, aimed at the professional market. It allows the user to tap into the intermediate frequency (IF) section of the scanner's circuit. Such sockets are normally used to allow the intermediate frequency waveform to be examined on test instruments such as oscilloscopes, and they also allow the signal to be processed in other ways for other modes such as SSB and telemetry. On the SX-400, the facility allows SSB to be resolved if a communications-type HF receiver is available. The output is merely taken to the HF receiver's aerial socket and the receiver is then tuned to 10.7 MHz (the SX-400's IF output frequency). By switching to SSB mode the HF receiver is then used merely as an IF amplifier/detector.

Operating your scanner 4

Some scanners are fairly easy to operate, others not so. Operation is a task that, often, is not helped when the instruction manual seems to be written in pidgin English — usually a strange cross between Japanese and Americanese. In my opinion, a classic example of a poorly written manual is that supplied with early SX-200s, which earned a reputation among owners as one of the most baffling documents ever produced. However, whatever the quality of instruction manual, the owner should at least *try* to understand it, as failure to know how the equipment works will at best frustrate the operation and at worst lead to serious damage.

Synthesised scanners

These fall into two distinct categories; internally and externally programmed. Internally programmed scanners are merely one step better than crystal controlled scanners, in that they are programmed to scan through a series of pre-selected channel frequencies and do no more than that. Indeed, the only real advantage over the crystal controlled type is; if you find a particular channel is not of great interest it is a simple matter to re-program the scanner without going to the expense of buying more crystals.

The externally programmed synthesised scanner offers far more versatility. Typical of this type are the Bearcats, SX series, Yaesu-Musen, Icom, etc. Normally these scanners not only allow scanning of normal pre-determined channels but also have search facilities.

Searching
Let us imagine a situation. You are not familiar with VHF or UHF communications but you have bought a synthesised scanner and although you know what you want to listen to, you are not sure what frequencies such transmissions are on in your area. For instance, you

may wish to monitor the transmissions from your local airport. A look at some bandplans such as those in Chapter 7 of this book will tell you that voice transmissions in the main aircraft band are located between 118 and 136 MHz and are transmitted in AM mode. Now you have a rough idea where to look but still no idea of the exact frequencies that you may want. On most synthesised scanners it should now be a fairly simple matter to find the frequencies you want although it may take a little patience. First, you need to get your scanner to *search* between 118 and 136 MHz. The handbook for your equipment will tell you how to set the limit of the lowest and highest frequency of the band you wish to hunt through. Depending on the set, you may also need to select AM mode reception although on some models, such as the Bearcats, AM will automatically be selected when you tune to these frequencies.

Once you have got the scanner searching it is merely a question of waiting until you hear the transmissions you want. As the scanner stops on such transmissions you must be ready to make a note of the channel frequency that is shown on the readout. You may require several such frequencies in the example we have given as, for instance, most airports of any size usually transmit on a number of frequencies; at least one for the approach controller and at least one for the control tower.

Once you have found and made a note of all the frequencies in the particular band you have been searching you should then stop the scanner and enter those frequencies into memory.

Memory scanning
Having searched for channel frequencies, found them and entered them into memory we then go on to true scanning: where the equipment is set to step, one by one, through each channel to see if anything is being transmitted.

For general listening it is likely that all the available channels will be scanned. However, there may be occasions when some channels are not required — possibly because they are very busy — and locking-on to them prevents hearing other channels that are of more interest. In this case it is possible to lock-out the unwanted channels. There are usually two methods of doing this. On scanners like the Bearcats and AORs it is possible to lock-out channels individually. This means that at any time a locked-out channel may be returned back into the scanning sequence. On other scanners, like the SX-200, it may not be possible to manipulate the channels individually. What happens is that two scanning sequences are set up. One, *scan A*, scans *all* the available memory channels. However, any of those channels can be designated as a secondary channel. In that case, *scan B* may be selected and any channel that has been designated as secondary will *not* be scanned. In other words you set up a complete bank of locked-out channels which is switched in or out of the scan sequence.

As a point of interest to newcomers, it's worth remembering that, very often, a transmission is encountered after it has started — you may even only hear the last word or two. What has happened is that the transmission was started while your scanner was checking through other channels. Also, bear in mind that while your scanner is monitoring one transmission you may well be missing another transmission on another channel. These may seem obvious but it is surprising how many scanner owners, initially at least, have some difficulty grasping these points.

Base stations

Most synthesised scanners are used as a base station, that is, permanently sited, rather than mobile as in a vehicle. There is no particular difficulty in setting up a base station installation, but do bear in mind the comments in Chapter 5 on aerials.

There are a few points to remember when locating the scanner. Always avoid places where there are extremes of temperature, moisture or dampness. It is also not advisable to locate the scanner in the vicinity of other equipment such as television sets. Strong electromagnetic fields around a TV can be picked up as an annoying buzz, by the scanner. Other forms of interference may also be a problem in certain locations — these are dealt with in more detail later in this chapter.

Mobile operation

Nearly all scanners can be used in a vehicle with a standard 13.8 volt supply with negative earth chassis. Most scanners are supplied with a bracket for this purpose and it is simply a question of fitting this bracket, with self-tapping screws, into a suitable location in the vehicle.

When deciding where to put the scanner in the vehicle take note of a few points. First, do not site it in front of hot air vents. The high temperature will certainly not do the scanner any good and, indeed, it may be high enough to damage any plastics that may have been used in the scanner's construction.

Second, note that unless you intend using an extension loudspeaker, you will need to make sure the scanner's loudspeaker is not obstructed. Most scanners only have about 1 watt audio output. In a quiet room that may seem more than adequate but it is barely enough in a car. An inexpensive external speaker can help tremendously (see Chapter 6, on accessories).

Finally, always bear in mind that there are thieves about. Not so many years ago specialised equipment such as scanners and amateur gear could be left in a vehicle because the average thief knew he would have little chance of selling it. Nowadays the situation has changed; there is a large and ready market. The answer to this is to either hide the scanner away or remove it althogether when the vehicle is left unattended. One way this can be done is by fitting the scanner to a sliding mount of the type often used for CB equipment. The mount, complete with scanner, can be removed in seconds and locked away in the boot, or even carried with you.

Portables (see photo page 151)

Until recently, the only portables available in Britain were the small, crystal controlled scanners and these usually fell into three categories: marine and 2 metre amateur band, aircraft band or dual-banders.

The 2 metre amateur band is between 144 and 146 MHz while the marine band between 156 and 162 MHz. These two bands are very close and so it is usually quite a simple matter to re-tune a scanner tuned to one band so that it receives the other band — always assuming, of course, that you replace the crystals with ones for the new frequencies. Circuit diagrams are supplied with most scanners and anyone with a reasonable ability to recognise the relevant parts of the circuit should know what to trim. But a word of warning to the non-technical. Should you upset trimming controls in other parts of the circuit it is virtually impossible to get the scanner working properly again, without specialist test equipment.

Choosing crystals

Most people, when buying a crystal controlled scanner, specify the channels they want to cover, at the time of purchase. However, an owner may later wish to change crystals, but this might not be as straightforward as it first appears.

Although crystals are remarkably stable (that is, they do not vary much in oscillating frequency), they rarely oscillate *exactly* at the specified frequency. In the scanner, small trimmer capacitors allow fine adjustment of crystal oscillation frequency to allow exact setting. Ideally crystal trimming is a job you should leave to an expert with measuring equipment, but if you are really stuck, it is possible to do it approximately by ear. Tune the scanner to a fairly weak signal and then adjust the trimmer for minimum background hiss or noise.

Should you want to get crystals for standard bands, eg, marine, amateur or aircraft bands, these can usually be bought, over the counter, from dealers. On the other hand, should you want to tune to other bands, you may need to specially order crystals. You also need to be sure of a number of other factors.

First, you must be sure that the scanner can cope with the bands you want to tune. For instance, it's no use trying to tune say 88 MHz on a scanner designed to operate solely at 144 MHz and above. The signal amplifying circuits just wouldn't be able to cope even if you re-trimmed them. The next thing you will need to know is the intermediate frequency of the scanner which on most scanners is 10.7 MHz. This information should be in the instruction manual, where you should also find details of what kind of crystal you will need. Crystals are rarely made to oscillate at the actual frequency required — they are usually made instead for a much lower frequency which, when multiplied by a specified whole number will give the wanted frequency. The tuning circuits in the scanner do the multiplying, but *you* need to know by what number. Your handbook will either say something like '5th overtone crystal' or will show a formula along the lines of: 'crystal = desired frequency minus 10.7, divided by 5.' You must let the crystal supplier have this information as well as whether the crystal operates in *series* or *parallel* mode which again will be specified in your handbook. If this information is not to hand you will have to go back to your dealer who should be able to supply it.

Ordering crystals

You need to know:

1 The required frequency minus the IF frequency.
2 Which overtone.
3 Series or parallel mode.

You may be able to order a crystal from your dealer but if not they can often be obtained through mail order companies who advertise in magazines aimed at the amateur radio market.

Using a portable

Portables are obviously intended to be carried around and a consequence of this is that a frequent shortcoming is the aerial, which must be small. It is usually a short telescopic aerial or even, in some cases, just a short length of loose wire terminated in a small jack plug. The latter often provides poor performance and if better range is required is best replaced by either a telescopic aerial or, a helical aerial (often referred to as a 'rubber duck'). Note, though, that the aerial used needs to be designed for the frequency that will be covered by the scanner — in other words a CB band aerial will not produce good results if the scanner is tuned to another band. For more specific information on this topic, refer to Chapter 5.

Whatever kind of portable is being used, the positioning of the aerial is important. A scanner carried in the pocket close to the body will have poor pick-up because the sheer mass of the body will upset the characteristics of the aerial and in some cases will screen it from signals. It is also important that the aerial is in what is known as the right polarisation 'plane': most communication signals at VHF and UHF are transmitted from vertically polarised aerials and so the scanner aerial needs to be vertically polarised, too. Where possible therefore, the scanner's aerial should be kept clear of the body and the aerial, usually, upright.

Portables in vehicles

There is no reason why a portable scanner can't be used in a vehicle, but don't expect good results if you are just using the portable's own aerial. Vehicle bodies provide a very effective screen, preventing good reception and so for best results an external aerial is necessary. One quick way of providing this facility is to use an aerial that has a magnetic base, so that it can be put in position and removed whenever desired, without the need to drill holes in the bodywork. Again, specific details are given in Chapter 5.

Power for the scanner can be either from the scanner's internal batteries, or from the vehicle's power circuit, through a suitable adaptor. Make sure the adaptor is the right one for the voltage required by the portable. Often scanner manufacturers will offer these adaptors, sometimes called 'power converters', as an optional accessory. Typically they consist of a small box of electronics with a lead at one end to plug into the scanner and a lead at the other end to plug into the vehicle's cigar lighter. A word of caution though on some other types. Many of the cheaper adaptors can draw quite heavy current — even when the scanner is not being used. So, if you intend to wire the adaptor permanently into the vehicle's power circuit you must be able to switch the adaptor off when you are not using the scanner, otherwise it will unnecessarily drain the vehicle's battery.

Beware — charger or supply

It is vitally important when connecting an external supply to a portable scanner that the supply is of the correct type, otherwise irreparable damage may occur to the scanner. Some scanners have a socket for an external supply, labelled something like 'DC 6V'. Other scanners may have a socket labelled 'charge'. Some scanners may have both, or different sockets.

DC supply
This socket is intended for you to run the set from a suitable direct current power source at the specified voltage. Some portables also have a small circuit built into them that will also use that current to charge internal cells. Your manual should tell you this.

Charge
This socket is *not* intended for an external supply. The re-chargeable cells in the scanner require a specially controlled re-charging current so that they charge up at the correct rate. Putting an uncontrolled current into this socket, even at the right voltage, will cause the cells to charge far too quickly and could damage them. In some instances this can also be a cause of overheating, which can damage other components in the scanner, too.

Polarity
If you intend using a mains adaptor that was not made by the scanner manufacturer you must ensure that the plug fitted to the adaptor is wired the same way round as the socket on the scanner. The fact that the adaptor has the right plug to fit the scanner's socket does not mean that the socket and plug's positive and negative contacts match.

Interference

Scanners, like a lot of other radio receivers, may be upset by various types of 'man-made' interference. Typical examples of interference sources are home appliances that contain electric motors, and home computers. When using your scanner in the home it is a good idea to keep it well away from such items. It is also advisable not to site your scanner on top of a television set which can also generate strong electromagnetic signals. Most interference sources in the home can be minimised — you can always turn the TV or vacuum cleaner off. On the other hand, users living close to industrial sites may find that nearby machinery causes persistent problems. There are several courses of action that can be taken.

First, make sure that your own installation is not inviting problems. A good, high, outside aerial sited well away from machinery and fed through good quality coaxial cable of the correct impedence (see Chapter 5) may well cure the problem. Many scanners have a connection on the rear apron for an earth and in some cases a wire connected between this point and a copper spike inserted into the ground may make a significant difference.

If this fails to resolve the problem then you may be faced with somewhat more drastic action. In most countries it is an offence to radiate strong signals from machinery which is not fitted with adequate suppression. In such cases it is usually advisable, if you are sure who the culprit is, to make a friendly and tactful approach and try and get the owner of the interference source to sort the problem out. If this fails then you can of course approach the necessary authority, which in the UK is the local post office, and ask them to investigate the matter. However, be warned that if you are complaining because someone is interfering with your *illegal* listening activities, then the authorities will take a very dim view of your complaint.

In the case of a base station, another source of interference may cause problems. Sometimes, persistent interference can be transmitted along mains wiring — there is quite an easy way to test for this. Obtain a battery of the required voltage and power the scanner off this source: in most cases a car battery will do nicely. If the scanner does not suffer from interference when run off the battery, then you know that the problem is being transmitted along the mains wiring and there are two ways that the interference can now be eliminated.

First, the scanner can be permanently run from batteries, but bear in mind that most synthesised scanners draw quite a heavy current. An automobile battery may be allright, but it will be necessary to recharge it when the scanner is not in use. If such batteries and a charger are available then obviously this is an easy way to tackle the problem. However, there is another and neater solution. It is possible to buy special interference eliminators that plug into a normal domestic supply socket. The most recent types consist of a small box with a plug on one side and matching socket on the other. They contain electronics to remove interference spikes from the domestic AC supply and, once plugged-in, the scanner's mains voltage adaptor is then plugged into the socket on the rear of the unit. Interference eliminators are often used, too, by computer users in cases where their computers suffer from mains-borne interference

Vehicle interference
All vehicles generate some level of interference from their electrical circuits and in some cases this can obliterate weak signals picked-up on a scanner in mobile use. Remember that mobile conditions are far from ideal anyway, and signals that are strong into a base station may well disappear below the level of vehicle ignition noise if some steps are not taken to reduce the problem.

Ignition noise
The first and most familiar type of interference, pulse noise, is caused by the vehicle's high tension ignition circuit. If this is excessive the first step is to fit a suppressor capacitor (specified for this type of interference) to the ignition coil. The coil will have three connections. The large thick

lead that goes to the distributor and two smaller leads, one marked 'CB' and the other 'SW'. The body clip of the suppressor capacitor must be connected to ground and the small flying lead must go to 'SW' (never connect to 'CB'). Ensure a good contact onto the chassis for the clip of the capacitor by scraping away any paintwork, rust, dirt, etc.

If this does not reduce interference to an acceptable level then you may need to replace the capacitor (if one exists) inside the distributor — it is not unknown for a capacitor to go open-circuit with age and no longer be effective.

You might never be able to completely eliminate this type of interference, but if it remains at a high level you should seek further advice from a garage.

If your vehicle is fitted with contactless electronic ignition you should refer to the vehicle handbook before attempting any kind of suppression. Some circuits of this type can cease to operate if fitted with capacitors.

Generator/alternator whine
As the name suggests this is a whining noise, heard through the receiver, that increases or decreases in pitch depending on the engine revs. It can get into the scanner in two ways; through the power supply lead or via the aerial.

It is simple to check which kind of problem is present by pulling out the aerial plug. If the sound persists then the interference is being transmitted along the power supply lead. A special device called an 'in-line choke' can be used to reduce this interference. Simple cut into the positive supply lead to the scanner and fit the choke in-line (they generally have simple screw connectors at both ends).

Often there is one further trick that sometimes dramatically reduces this kind of interference. Often the problem may be resolved by installing a power line to the scanner direct from the battery's positive terminal, by-passing the car's existing electrical wiring. The only problem that can arise is that if you leave the vehicle long enough and forget to switch the scanner off, then it will drain the battery.

If generator/alternator interference is entering the scanner via the aerial then a different kind of action is called for. In the case of a generator, a simple suppressor capacitor may be connected between the chassis and the generator's output lead. Note that you will need a capacitor designed for the job. In the case of an alternator, the solution really depends on the make and it is best to consult your car agent. The method of suppression is usually similar to that for a generator, particularly in the case of Lucas, Bosch and Delco types where the flying lead of the capacitor is connected to the terminal marked 'IND'.

Other interference

Instruments and equipment fitted in modern cars are usually quite well suppressed. However, older models may present interference problems from a variety of sources including: screen wiper motors, voltage regulators, instrument stabilisers, heater motor, indicator lights and stop lights. The most common cause of interference is the wiper motor; which, fortunately, is quite easy to identify — for obvious reasons. Often a simple solution to the problem is to connect a wire between the metal body of the motor and the chassis of the car (many of these motors 'float' on rubber buffers).

As for the other sources of interference mentioned, then specialist suppliers can provide the necessary suppressors specially designed for the job. In the UK the nearest dealer for Lucus parts can supply a wide range of suppressors. Lucus manufactures a device to suit virtually every kind of suppression problem.

General tips

One further method of reducing interference is known as 'bonding'. Many cars often have poor electrical contact between the engine bonnet and the engine compartment. This could mean that the bonnet does not screen all interference generated around the engine. A cure for this can be to use a bonding strap, consisting of copper braid. One end is connected to the chassis and the other to the bonnet (usually onto one of the bolts that holds the hinge mechanism). However, the strap *must* connect onto good, clean, bared metal, to give perfect electrical contact.

Sometimes, taking one step to reduce interference appears to have little effect. However, do not undo the work you have done. Carry on adding other methods of suppression. The real trick to 'quietening your car down' is to carry out steps that reduce the noise, little by little. It is rare that there is any 'miracle cure' where fitting one suppressor suddenly solves all your problems.

Flutter

This is not actually interference, but can be a problem with mobile working. The effect is a fluttering in the strength of the received signal. The biggest cause of this effect is the aerial swinging around on the vehicle. As the whip moves in relation to the body of the car its sensitivity to radio signals changes. The only real cure for this is to use a very stiff aerial. Swishy whip aerials may look very flash, but can cause terrible flutter.

Scanner tricks

Some synthesised scanners such as some Bearcat models can be made to tune outside their normal tuning ranges. Tricks like this are not really necessary with full coverage scanners such as the AORs, Yaesu and Icom but can be very useful with those receivers which do not cover certain frequencies.

However, although it is possible to trick some sets into working outside their normal range, it should be remembered that the further out of range they go then the more the sensitivity starts to fall off. This is because the tuning and amplifying circuits were not designed for this coverage.

Details of the Bearcat 220 and 250 are given here but I must scotch a rumour about the SX-200. This scanner cannot be made to receive outside its quoted coverage. I know this for a fact because I have actually been able to get my own SX-200 to appear as if it was tuning out of range . . . in other words the frequency readout showed that it was. I will not bother to explain the procedure to achieve this because it is pointless. What happens is that, although the oscillator tuning circuits will go out of range, the moment this happens the signal amplifying stages switch off. It would appear that the internal microproccessor is programmed to switch-in one of the three signal amplifying heads, VHF low, VHF high and UHF, depending on where the set is tuned. However any attempt to get the synthesiser tuning out of range results in none of the amplifier heads being brought into circuit.

However, some trickery is available on two Bearcat models.

Bearcat 220FB

The gaps not covered by this scanner are 50–66 MHz, 80–118 MHz, 136–144 MHz and 174–420 MHz. The latter gap covers such a wide range that the receiver will not operate over its entire span even when tricked into coverage. However, the other gaps can be easily covered with the following procedure. We will take the first gap, 50–66 MHz as an example and you only need to substitute the other figures for the other gaps.

Use MANUAL to find a spare memory channel and then:

(1) Press 50   (5) Press LIMIT
(2) Press E   (6) Press SEARCH (ignore the ERROR signal)
(3) Press LIMIT   (7) Press LIMIT
(4) Press 66   (8) Press SEARCH

The scanner will now start to search upwards from 50 MHz.

Bearcat 250

A similar type of method is used to fill gaps in the coverage of the 250FB scanner. For instance this set does not normally cover the amateur 2 m band but will with the following sequence.

Find a clear or spare memory channel. Make sure the squelch is closed and then:

(1) Press 146
(2) Press LIMIT
(3) Press 146
(4) Press LIMIT
(5) Press STORE
(6) Open and close the squelch
(7) Press MANUAL

(8) Press 174
(9) Press LIMIT
(10) Press 174
(11) Press LIMIT
(12) Press SEARCH
(13) Press RECALL
(14) Press SEARCH

The set should search downwards in frequency from 146 to 133 MHz.

To store a frequency, open the squelch just before reaching it and use the search button to step onto the frequency. Then, with the squelch still open switch the scanner off and then on again. The frequency should be stored in the appropriate memory.

SX-200

Having already said that it is not possible to carry out a similar procedure with the SX-200, there is a simple little sequence for this set which gets rid of the persistent clock. Owners of the SX-200 will know that this wretched clock is a nuisance when trying to monitor a single channel. Instead of the frequency being displayed the time pops up. It can be got rid of by a trick search process. Enter the frequency you want, press the LIMIT button, enter the frequency again and then press the SEARCH button. The set now tries to search between the two frequencies and as a result shows the same frequency all the time, albeit with a very slight flicker.

SX-400

Despite its impressive facilities and performance, the SX-400 does not have facilities for single sideband. However, it does have a socket on the back with 10.7 MHz IF output, and if an HF communications type receiver is available then this can be used as an SSB IF strip. Simply connect the IF output to the antenna socket of the HF receiver and tune it to 10.7 MHz. Turn the volume down on the scanner and listen on the HF set whilst tuning on the scanner.

Aerials 5

The terms 'aerial' and 'antenna' are synonymous, meaning that part of a radio system which radiates electromagnetic energy (a transmitting aerial) or picks-up electromagnetic energy (receiving aerial). An aerial, together with connecting cable, supports, etc, is known as an aerial system.

Forget the telescopic

Most scanners are provided with a telescopic aerial which is only of use to enable the scanner to receive strong transmissions from a nearby transmitter. To get the best out of your equipment and to be able to receive weaker transmissions you will need to invest in a proper aerial system — and why not? You have probably invested quite a considerable amount of hard-earned cash in your scanner and so it would be a shame not to get the best out of it just for the sake of a few more pounds. A reasonable aerial system does not need to cost a great deal of money.

When an external aerial is used the telescopic must be removed

Leaving the telescopic aerial plugged-in when also using an external aerial will upset the input stages of the scanner and the resulting mismatch will spoil reception. So, whenever you use an external aerial with your scanner, remember to disconnect the telescopic aerial.

VHF/UHF aerials

The use of aerials is something of a black art for the newcomer to VHF/UHF radio and the situation is not helped by the fact that there are a great many types to choose from. They basically fall, however, into two distinct types; broadband or narrow band.

Before proceeding further, though, we should consider some of the basic principles of VHF/UHF aerial design because they vary greatly from those of aerials used at HF and lower frequencies. For instance, one common myth amongst many non-technical people is that 'the bigger the aerial the better'. It is not unknown for some first time scanner buyers to try and improve reception by using long lengths of wire with one end poked into the scanner's aerial socket. Not only will this not improve reception but will probably produce even poorer results than the simple telescopic aerial. The simple reason for this is that at VHF/UHF frequencies, aerials must be of the correct dimensions. A typical example, will be familar to most people, is the UHF television aerial. Notice how the width of the aerials in your area are all pretty much the same — the length varies according to the number of elements on the boom of the aerial but the width remains constant. That is because they are all tuned to pick up the same transmitter.

Polarisation (Figures 5.1 and 5.2)

Having considered the importance of physical dimensions of aerials we must also consider polarisation. The 'quarter-wave' whip example is typical of a vertically polarised aerial. All that means is that the whip or main element of the aerial is upright and, in practice, will only be suitable for receiving signals from aerials which are also vertically polarised. Some types of aerial, though, are horizontally polarised. They operate in a plane that is parallel to the ground. These are rarely used for mobile communications as they are directional and literally have to be pointed

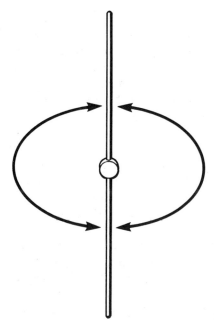

Figure 5.1 Vertical polarisation. Pick up pattern is in all directions.

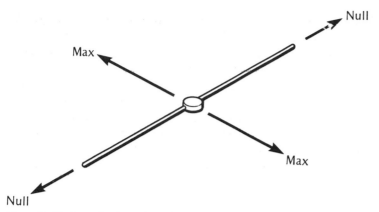

Figure 5.2 Horizontal polarisation. The antenna is sensitive in two directions on and picks up very little end-on.

at the signal source. Horizontally polarised aerials are frequently used for comunications between two fixed points.

Virtually all aerial designs can be used vertically polarised but some designs, such as quarter-wave whips and 'discones', do not readily lend themselves to horizontal operation. There are some other forms of polarisation, namely 'slant' and 'circular', but these rarely apply to scanners and so are not dealt with here.

Narrow band aerials

Whips (Figure 5.3)

Let us now look at practical designs of whips. First, the quarter-wave whip. It is essentially a narrow band aerial although in fact, in reception, will operate with fair performance over a wide range of frequencies. For instance, an aerial cut for 100 MHz will provide reasonable reception from about 50 to 200 MHz. It is difficult to quote exact figures as a lot will depend on the strength of the signals in a given area.

The quarter-wave whip aerial lends itself to both mobile and base station use. Commercially available mobile whip aerial systems are usually sold in two parts: the whip itself which is cut by the purchaser to whatever length required and a mounting unit. The mounting unit can take the form of a 'through body mounting', fitted in a similar way to a normal car radio aerial system. Another mounting unit consists of a small clamp, attached to the water drain gutter above the car doors. This fitting obviously means that no holes have to be drilled in the car's bodywork. The need for drilling is again avoided when a magnetically-mounted aerial system is used, consisting of a large, powerful magnet covered in a rubber boot, on top of which is a small clamp to which the whip is connected. Such 'magmounts' are very popular these days

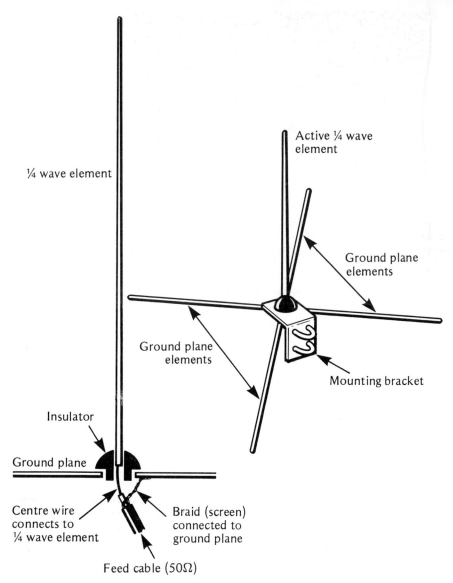

¼ wave element

Active ¼ wave
element

Ground plane
elements

Ground plane
elements

Mounting bracket

Insulator

Ground plane

Centre wire
connects to
¼ wave element

Braid (screen)
connected to
ground plane

Feed cable (50Ω)

Figure 5.3 Whip antenna. The ground plane can be a steel car body or in the case of a base aerial can be ¼ wave long rods.

because they can easily be removed when the car is left unattended. This means the aerial is not at the mercy of vandals and it is not so obvious that valuable scanning equipment is installed.

In the case of mobile operation, the body of the car provides the 'ground plane', necessary for correct quarter-wave whip aerial functioning. In the case of a base aerial a ground plane is provided, usually, by four elements, each a quarter-wave or more in length.

Photograph 5(a) Typical ground plane aerial. This one is designed for airband and the 'drooping' radials give a better 50 Ohm match.

Dimensions

Remember, in Chapter 2, we saw that for any given radio frequency signal there is a corresponding wavelength. Well, when we talk of a quarter-wave aerial we are referring to the physical size of an aerial which is one quarter of the wavelength of the operating frequency. In practice, the whip length is around 5 per cent less. There is a simple mathematical formula to work this out: Quarter-wave aerial length = 71.5 divided by frequency (in MHz).

The resulting length is in metres. The story does not quite end there, because in order for the aerial to perform correctly it should have a ground plane. In the case of a base aerial this usually comprises metal rods connected to the earthing braid of the aerial cable at the base of the whip. In the case of mobile operation, the earthed metal bodywork of the vehicle acts as the ground plane.

In addition to the quarter-wave whip there are several variants, notably the $\frac{5}{8}$ wave whips fitted with appropriate load coils.

Dipoles

The dipole (which also forms the basis of the Yagi aerial — see later) is the most commonly used aerial at VHF/UHF frequencies. It can take two forms; simple or folded. It is not normally used as a mobile aerial because of the difficulties of mounting it. However, it is used extensively as a base station aerial and, unlike the whip, does not require a ground plane as such.

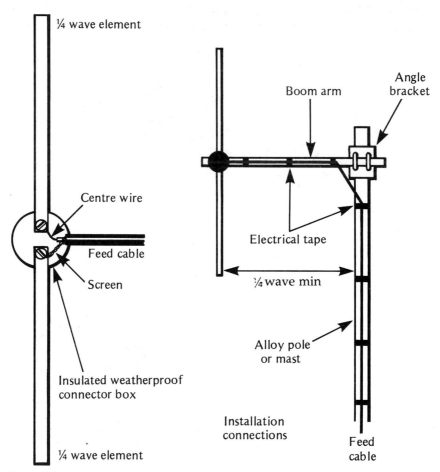

Figure 5.4 The dipole. Vertically polarised it provides good all round reception.

Let us look at a simple dipole which consists of just two elements, the active and the passive. Refer to Figure 5.4 and you will see that what we have, in effect, is two quarter-wave elements, one above the other. The dipole therefore is a half wavelength across. It can be mounted vertically polarised, which makes it omni-directional or horizontally polarised which makes it directional into two areas. Most scanner users, though, find the vertical version the most useful. The calculations for each element are the same as those given for the quarter wave-whip.

A variation on the simple dipole is known as the folded dipole where the outer ends of the two elements are looped across and connected to each other.

Yagis (Figure 5.5)

The Yagi is a dipole (usually folded) which has added elements to make it directional. Most television aerials are of Yagi construction. The folded dipole is mounted on a boom with a reflector element behind and

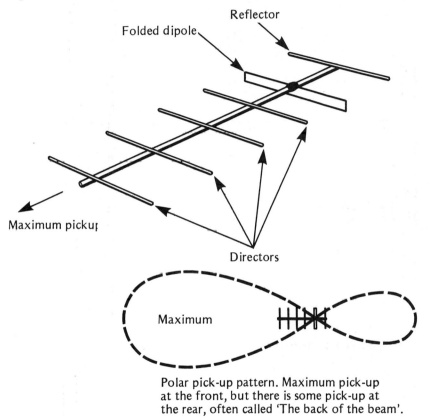

Folded dipole

Reflector

Maximum pickup

Directors

Maximum

Polar pick-up pattern. Maximum pick-up at the front, but there is some pick-up at the rear, often called 'The back of the beam'.

Figure 5.5 The Yagi (beam).

director elements in front. The directional characteristic of the aerial and its gain varies according to the number of director elements. Yagi aerials are normally used for working between two fixed points and can be used either vertically or horizontally. Amateurs use Yagis for reception of long range VHF/UHF transmissions, but to do so successfully have to fit them with motorised aerial rotators; so the aerial can be pointed exactly at the transmitting aerial.

Photograph 5(b) An eight element Yagi operating in horizontal polarisation mode. The antenna is highly directional hence the rotator motor to turn it.

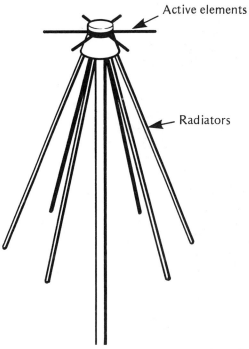

Figure 5.6 The Discone. Despite the horizontal top elements the aerial is vertically polarised and very broadband.

Broadband aerials

Discones (Figure 5.6)

This is the aerial of the greatest interest to the scanner owner who wants to tune over a wide range of frequencies. It is a very broadband aerial and some types will work quite effectively over the entire VHF/UHF bands.

It is not an aerial that readily lends itself to being home-made as it is quite complex in terms of the metalwork involved. It will only work as a vertically polarised aerial and is only really suitable as the basis of a base station aerial system. Commercially there are a number to choose from and prices range quite widely. However, as a simple guide it is best to go for one that has a large number of elements and preferably elements that are made of solid rod or seamless tube. Those made from thin seamed alloy tend to deteriorate very quickly in poor weather.

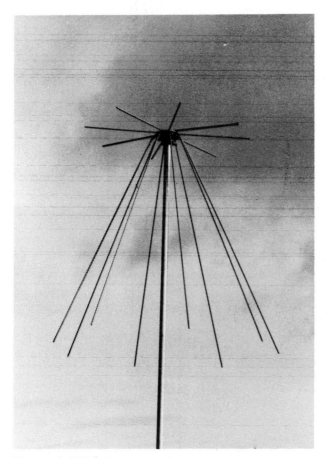

Photograph 5(c) The Discone. Easily the most popular broadband aerial amongst scanner users.

Aerials for portables

A hand-portable scanner can be used with virtually any type of mobile or base aerial and the consequent performance will be better than any small aerial that is normally attached directly to the scanner. However, use of such aerials defeats the portability feature of the scanner.

Some portable scanners are supplied with only a small length of wire to act as an aerial. These are probably the poorest aerials as they can rarely be kept in an upright position. A far better choice is the use of a telescopic or helical, and to this end most portable scanners have a socket frequently either a BNC type or miniature jack plug for an external aerial. By far the most common aerial used on portable scanners is the following.

Helicals (rubber ducks)

A helical aerial comprises a metal spring, shrouded in rubber or plastic. They are often seen on walkie-talkies and offer the advantage that unlike a telescopic they are flexible and not easily broken. In practice, the spring usually consists of a metal wire of $\frac{5}{8}$th wavelength wound over a width of about 10 mm. The top part is stretched out slightly but often the lower end is fairly close wound so as to provide correct impedance matching with the scanner.

Helicals offer better performance than the loose wire aerial, are very compact and portable, do not easily break and, being far shorter than

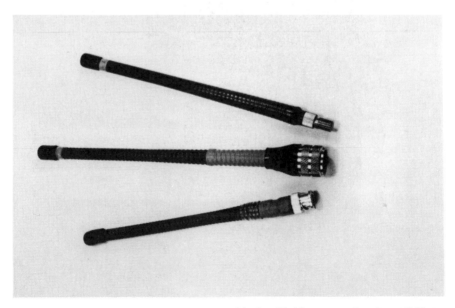

Photograph 5(d) Helicals or 'Rubber Ducks'. Ideal for hand held scanners, they are available with BNC PL259 and screw-in connectors.

respective telescopic aerials, are less likely to do personal damage like poking someone's eye out. However, it is likely that a telescopic aerial will give better performance.

Whatever kind of aerial is used, remember that if the scanner is kept in a pocket or any other position close to the body the performance will be reduced. Not only does the body act as a screen but the sheer mass can upset the aerial impedance. Portable scanners do not work very well inside vehicles or buildings. In each case it should be possible to attach an external aerial to the set to improve performance. In the case of mobile operation a magnetically mounted aerial is ideal.

Satellite aerials

Although reception of many satellite transmissions can easily be accomplished on fairly simple VHF/UHF equipment it presents a special problem in terms of aerials. Remember how earlier we discussed the problem of polarisation when we said that the transmitting and

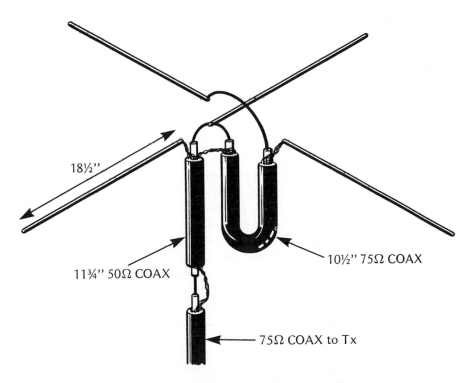

18½"

11¾" 50Ω COAX

10½" 75Ω COAX

75Ω COAX to Tx

Figure 5.7 The feed arrangements for a 2m crossed dipole antenna. Each of the elements is 18½inches long.

receiving aerials must be phased the same way. The problem we face with satellite reception is that the satellite itself will not have an aerial that remains in the same phase. Orbiting satellites travel from horizon to horizon and their aerials will change position and vary in phase in relation to the aerial on the ground.

The effect of this is that signals from a satellite will appear to get louder and then slowly fade away before getting louder again and then again fading. The way to overcome this is to use what is known as a crossed dipole — effectively two dipoles with the resultant aerial having horizontal *and* vertical polarisation (Figure 5.7).

Simple and inexpensive crossed dipoles can be bought from Halbar Aerials and Jay-Beam, whose addresses are at the back of the book.

Cable

All base and mobile aerials need to be connected to the scanner using screened coaxial cable. However, any old cable that you have lying around might not be suitable. There are several types of coaxial cable available, some for aerials, other for audio and hi-fi use. The latter are unsuitable as are cables designed for use with a normal car radio.

The remaining aerial cables fall into two sections, 50 ohm and 75 ohm impedance types. Cable impedance is most critical. The 50 ohm variety is normally used to connect professional, commercial, amateur and CB aerials while 75 ohm cable is used for domestic VHF radio and television. You must use the right one for your scanner. The scanner instruction manual should tell you which cable impedence to use. Failing that the aerial socket on the set may be labelled with the impedence. If it is not shown then it is reasonably safe to assume that the correct cable is the 50 ohm type. A few older scanners do have 75 ohm inputs and in that case normal domestic TV coaxial cable can be used.

50 ohm cable is available from amateur and CB radio dealers but like the 75 ohm types two main kinds are available; normal or low-loss. If the scanner is only being used for VHF reception and only about 8 or 10 metres of cable is to be used then normal cable can be used. However, if UHF reception or long cable lengths are required then low loss cable is needed.

Cable construction
Whatever kind of coaxial cable you use, it will have roughly the construction shown in Figure 5.8. Starting at the middle is the core wire which carries the signal, shrouded in a plastic insulator. The insulator prevents the core from touching the outer braid, which is wound in such a way as to provide an earthed screen for the core. This screen serves two purposes: it ensures that the correct impedance is maintained along the

entire length of the cable; it stops any interference from reaching the inner core. Finally, the entire cable is covered in plastic insulation. It is important when installing an aerial that this outer insulation is intact and not torn or gouged so that the braid is exposed. Rainwater getting into the cable in such circumstances will almost certainly ruin the cable.

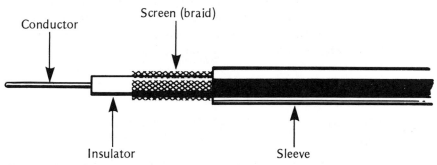

Figure 5.8 Coaxial cable.

As the screen of the cable is earthed, it is important when connecting the cable to either the aerial or the connector plug that the inner wire and the braid wire *never touch*. If they do, the incoming signal is earthed, and so lost.

Photograph 5(e) Simple crossed dipole for satellite reception. This one was made up from two old band 1 TV aerials. Note the phasing stub taped to the mast.

Connectors

In order to plug the aerial cable into the scanner you will need appropriate connectors. If you intend to fit your own then note that you will need a soldering iron: twisted wires or wires poked into sockets will

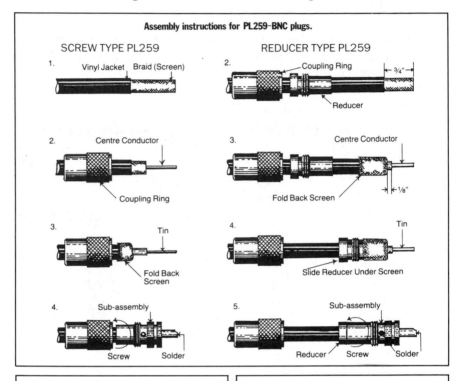

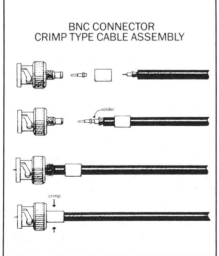

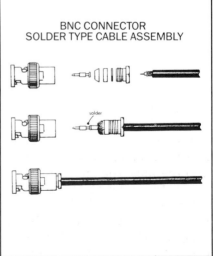

Figure 5.9 Various plugs and connectors.

almost certainly lead to signal losses. Several types of plug are in common use and are shown in Figure 5.9. It is also possible to purchase adaptors so that an aerial which has one type of plug can be connected to a scanner which takes another type.

PL259

Commonly found on CB sets and amateur equipment, PL259 connectors are only occasionally encountered on scanners, usually of the older variety. However, they are used extensively to connect to aerials. For instance a socket for a PL259 plug will be found on the base of most discones.

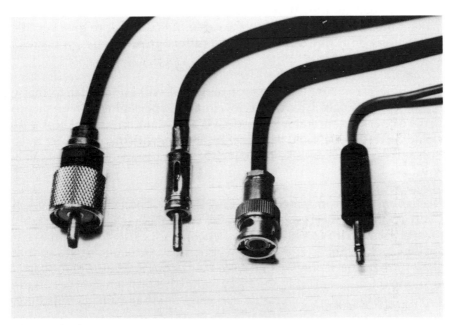

Photograph 5(f) Typical aerial plugs found on scanners. From left to right: PL259, Motorola, BNC and miniature jack. The latter is usually confined to hand held sets.

The plug comes in several varieties some of which are easier to fit than others. The simplest are designed for use with the thinner, standard (non-low-loss), cable. The cable is trimmed, about a quarter inch of braid is left and folded back over the outer insulator. The cable is then pushed into the plug and the braiding and insulator screwed into the plug's shell. Once fully home, the centre conductor is then soldered.

Other types of PL259 have a separate inner sleeve which is either a wide or narrow type depending on the coaxial cable used. This type of plug can be fitted to thicker, low-loss, cables and the appropriate sleeve is purchased separately. When fitting, the braid must be worked back over the sleeve. The inner conductor is then soldered in the normal way.

It is a good idea with both types of plug to expose more centre conductor than is needed. The surplus can be snipped off after soldering.

PL259 plugs have an outer shell that is internally threaded and when mated with the socket this shell is screwed up tight to ensure firm contact.

BNC

This connector is found on professional communication and test equipment and is much smaller than the PL259. However, it has a simple twist and pull action for release which makes it a lot quicker to change over than the PL259. This type of plug is used on some of the later scanners such as the AOR's. Unfortunately, its smaller dimensions make it more fiddly to attach to the cable. It is difficult to give specific instructions on fitting as construction differs greatly between makes.

Motorola

This is the car radio aerial type of plug that will be familiar to many people. Surprisingly in a way this low quality type of plug (low quality in terms of performance at VHF and UHF) is found on several scanners including the SX200N and Bearcats. Types vary with manufacturer but a look at the plug will usually make it clear how it is attached to the cable.

Miniature jack

A plug that is far from suited to VHF/UHF but it is occasionally found on some of the smaller portable crystal controlled scanners: probably chosen because it is small and very cheap. A look inside will make it obvious as to what is soldered to where, but a difficulty arises in that most miniature jack plugs do not have a big enough opening in the barrel to take 50 ohm coaxial cable. One way round this problem is to cut off the back end of the barrel with say, a hacksaw, so leaving a bigger opening.

Building an aerial

If you are not prepared to go to the expense of purchasing an expensive aerial such as a discone, it is possible to build a simple dipole, easily and cheaply. The job is made easier if you can lay your hands on an old Band 1 (BBC 405-line) TV aerial. A surprising number of these aerials still sit around in lofts unused in these days of UHF TV. If it *has* only been used inside then it will not have suffered from corrosion and will be eminently suitable for modification.

First unbolt the connector block from the boom and undo the nuts that hold the dipole elements. If the dipole is a folded type discard the loop and use either the directors or reflector to make up the new dipole elements. Use the aerial dimensions table given in Table 5.1 as a guide

Table 5.1 Element length guide for 1/4 and 5/8 loaded wave whips

MHz	1/4 mm	1/4 inch	5/8 mm	5/8 inch	MHz	1/4 mm	1/4 inch	5/8 mm	5/8 inch
25	2860	112.00	7150	280.0	315	226	8.91	565	22.2
30	2383	93.60	5957	234.0	320	223	8.77	557	21.9
35	2042	80.20	5105	200.0	325	220	8.64	550	21.6
40	1787	70.20	4467	175.0	330	216	8.50	540	21.2
45	1588	62.40	3970	156.0	335	213	8.38	532	20.9
50	1430	56.10	3575	140.0	340	210	8.25	525	20.6
55	1300	51.00	3250	127.0	345	207	8.13	517	20.3
60	1191	46.80	2977	117.0	350	204	8.02	510	20.0
65	1100	43.20	2750	108.0	355	201	7.90	502	19.7
70	1021	40.10	2552	100.0	360	198	7.80	495	19.5
75	953	37.40	2382	93.6	365	195	7.69	487	19.2
80	893	35.10	2232	87.7	370	193	7.58	482	18.9
85	841	33.00	2102	82.5	375	190	7.48	475	18.7
90	794	31.20	1985	78.0	380	188	7.38	470	18.4
95	752	29.50	1880	73.8	385	185	7.29	462	18.2
100	715	28.00	1787	70.2	390	183	7.20	457	18.0
105	680	26.70	1700	66.8	395	181	7.10	452	17.7
110	650	25.50	1625	63.8	400	178	7.02	445	17.5
115	621	24.40	1552	61.0	405	176	6.93	440	17.3
120	595	23.40	1487	58.5	410	174	6.84	435	17.1
125	572	22.40	1430	56.1	415	172	6.76	430	16.9
130	550	21.60	1375	54.0	420	170	6.68	425	16.7
135	529	20.80	1322	52.0	425	168	6.60	420	16.5
140	510	20.00	1275	50.1	430	166	6.53	415	16.3
145	493	19.30	1232	48.4	435	164	6.45	410	16.1
150	476	18.70	1190	46.8	440	162	6.38	405	15.9
155	461	18.10	1152	45.2	445	160	6.31	400	15.7
160	446	17.50	1115	43.8	450	158	6.24	395	15.6
165	433	17.00	1082	42.5	455	157	6.17	392	15.4
170	420	16.50	1050	41.2	460	155	6.10	387	15.2
175	408	16.00	1020	40.1	465	153	6.03	382	15.0
180	397	15.60	992	39.0	470	152	5.97	380	14.9
185	386	15.10	965	37.9	475	150	5.91	375	14.7
190	376	14.70	940	36.9	480	148	5.85	370	14.6
195	366	14.40	915	36.0	485	147	5.78	367	14.4
200	357	14.00	892	35.1	490	145	5.73	362	14.3
205	348	13.60	870	34.2	495	144	5.67	360	14.1
210	340	13.30	850	33.4	500	143	5.61	357	14.0

Table 5.1 *continued*

	1/4		5/8			1/4		5/8	
MHz	*mm*	*inch*	*mm*	*inch*	*MHz*	*mm*	*inch*	*mm*	*inch*
215	332	13.00	830	32.6	505	141	5.56	352	13.9
220	325	12.70	812	31.9	510	140	5.50	350	13.7
225	317	12.40	792	31.2	515	138	5.45	345	13.6
230	310	12.20	775	30.5	520	137	5.40	342	13.5
235	304	11.90	760	29.8	525	136	5.34	340	13.3
240	297	11.70	742	29.2	530	134	5.29	335	13.2
245	291	11.40	727	28.6	535	133	5.24	332	13.1
250	286	11.20	715	28.0	540	132	5.20	330	13.0
255	280	11.00	700	27.5	545	131	5.15	327	12.8
260	275	10.80	687	27.0	550	130	5.10	325	12.7
265	269	10.50	672	26.4	555	128	5.05	320	12.6
270	264	10.40	660	26.0	560	127	5.01	317	12.5
275	260	10.20	650	25.5	565	126	4.96	315	12.4
280	255	10.00	637	25.0	570	125	4.92	312	12.3
285	250	9.85	625	24.6	575	124	4.88	310	12.2
290	246	9.68	615	24.2	580	123	4.84	307	12.1
295	242	9.51	605	23.7	585	122	4.80	305	12.0
300	238	9.36	595	23.4	590	121	4.75	302	11.8
305	234	9.20	585	23.0	595	120	4.71	300	11.7
310	230	9.05	575	22.6	600	119	4.68	297	11.7

and, with a hacksaw, cut the two elements to the required dimensions. For general purpose listening elements of a length corresponding to a frequency 100 MHz are suitable but for specific reception of such bands as marine, air, etc, just cut to the appropriate length for that frequency. Drill the cut ends and re-fit the elements to the connector block. With the rest of the elements removed, the boom can now be re-used by bolting the block to one end of the tube. All that is needed now is cable and a clamp to hold the boom to a mast.

Fitting the cable is easy — just remember to make sure that the inner core goes to the element that points upwards.

Mounting external aerials

A whole range of fittings and mounting kits is available for installing aerials and you local TV aerial erection firm should be only too happy to sell you poles, fixing kits, etc. If you are lucky, the same firm may also

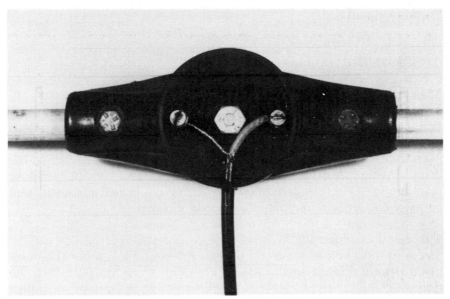

Photograph 5(g) The dipole's connector block prior to fitting to the boom arm. Note that for vertical use the element connected to the Coax cable's braid must be the one that points downwards.

have a pile of old scrap aerials and these, if they have not suffered too much from weathering, can provide a useful source of connector blocks and elements.

There are four basic ways of mounting an aerial outside and the corresponding kits are:

1 Wall mounting. This consists of a plate with brackets to hold a mounting pole. A drill capable of drilling into brick or masonry will be needed and expanding bolts should be used to retain the plate.
2 Eaves mounting. A smaller version of the wall mounting version, it is used with wood screws to fix onto the eaves. Note, though, that this method is only suitable for small lightweight aerials: even a small aerial can put considerable strain on its mountings during high winds.
3 Chimney lashing. The method often used for TV aerials, comprising one or two brackets held to a chimney by wire cable. Although easy to fit, it places the aerial in close proximity to the heat and smoke from the chimney which may accelerate the inevitable corrosion of the aerial.
4 Free standing mast. This is the most expensive solution but usually the best if you can afford it. An aluminium mast of 6 metres or more in length is partially sunk into the ground and held upright with wire guys. This mounting method can improve performance remarkably at some locations as it allows the aerial to be sited away from obstructions and above the level of trees and buildings that block signals. Planning permission may be required for this kind of installation.

Aerial amplifiers

Also known as RF or antenna amplifiers, signal boosters, etc. These devices fall into two categories:

Masthead amplifiers
These units consist of a small-signal amplifier housed in a weatherproof box, close to the aerial. They are useful for making-up for the signal losses that occur when long cables are used between the aerial and the scanner. DC current to power the unit is fed up the centre core of the coaxial cable — as the signal comes down, the DC goes up, without interference. One new variant on this theme is a broadband aerial that actually has an aerial amplifier built into its base.

Cable-end amplifiers
These connect between the end of the cable and the scanner. They are often powered by a small battery although some do plug into the domestic AC supply. Cable-end amplifiers have limitations as, unlike masthead amplifiers, they cannot improve a poor signal-to-noise ratio of an aerial system.

When to use an amplifier
In the ideal circumstances, that is, with an aerial of sufficient quality and short enough cable, an aerial amplifier is not needed. While capable of boosting weaker signals an aerial amplifier can also cause problems. For instance, strong signals received on other frequencies are also boosted and may overload the scanner.

However, some scanner users may live in areas where they are screened by high buildings or land, or may not be able to fit an aerial of sufficiently high quality. In such circumstances an amplifier *may* help. It may also be of use where long cable runs are necessary between the scanner and the aerial.

As a caution, users are advised to seek expert advice *before* installing an aerial amplifier, as wrongly doing so will cause more problems than it solves.

Accessories 6

Power supplies

Most non-portable scanners are supplied with a mains adaptor. Often these just consist of a small box with two leads, one going to the mains supply, the other going to the scanner. Some scanners such as the Bearcat 220FB have the circuit built-in. Whatever the scanner, the only time a scanner owner should need to buy an adaptor is perhaps if the original is lost or damaged. Some care must be taken in choosing a replacement and this warning also applies to the smaller mobile scanners and portable scanners which are not provided with an adaptor.

Some scanners have a certain amount of built-in voltage regulation and are tolerant of fairly wide DC input voltages, typically 12 V to 17 V. However others are more sensitive to higher voltages and damage could result if the incorrect voltage is applied.

Regulated or unregulated?
Ideally it is best to avoid unregulated supplies, in which output voltage is not stabilised and can be quite high if the current drawn by the scanner is low. Such power supplies are also more likely to cause mains hum interference. I give this warning in the knowledge that many adaptors supplied with scanners are unregulated. What must be borne in mind is that the manufacturer has usually carefully chosen the transformer so that it gives the right voltage under the load imposed by the scanner. Unless you are absolutely sure the replacement adaptor will do the same, play safe and stick to a regulated one.

Regulated supplies of 13.8 V are very much standard these days and usually available for quite modest prices from scanner, amateur and CB dealers. You will need a unit capable of supplying sufficient current — for most scanners 1 amp should be more than adequate. A power supply capable of supplying higher current than the scanner requires will not harm the scanner.

Warnings

Never, under any circumstances, use a transformer designed for electric trains or cars.

Be very careful about connecting the supply polarity the right way round. Full details on this are given in Chapter 4

Batteries

Most portable scanners are supplied with re-chargeable cells of the Ni-Cad type. Refer to Chapter 4 for specific details of charging these cells and note that you must *never* attempt to re-charge normal cells as they are likely to explode!

Ni-Cad cells have a limited lifetime (a minimum of 500 recharge cycles) and, occasionally, it may be necessary to replace them. If they are standard sizes: A, AA, C, D, etc, this presents little problem as they are now widely available, not only from radio/electrical dealers, but also from such outlets as photography shops, etc. Some scanners, though, have non-standard cells designed to fit within a certain space. Some of these can be quite different to obtain, particularly those used in some older models of scanner. If you are not able to obtain replacements from a scanner dealer then it is worth trying a hobby or model shop. Some cells used in radio controlled models are quite compact and can be joined together to give the required voltage. It's worth a try if you are desperate.

Loudspeakers/headphones

Loudspeakers

The loudspeaker built-in to most scanners, particularly portables, is very much of a compromise and audio output quality can usually be improved considerably by using an external loudspeaker. A larger loudspeaker than the one fitted to the scanner will often also provide louder output and this can be particularly useful in something like a noisy vehicle such as a van or lorry.

Suitable loudspeakers are available at reasonable prices from firms who stock CB equipment and chances are that such a loudspeaker will be fitted with a small jack plug which will match the socket on a lot of scanners. The loudspeaker should be of the correct impedance but this is not usually a problem as most sets will feed either 8 or 16 ohm loudspeakers and these are standard types.

I use a pair of small loudspeakers sold for use with 'Walkman' type personal cassette players. The three-pole stereo plug was removed and each lead was replaced with normal two-pole jacks. The pair of speakers were cheap, yet the 75 mm units give good clear audio output quality when used with a small portable scanner.

Photograph 6(a) A small speaker designed for use with personal stereo cassette players can be fitted with a suitable plug and makes a good and inexpensive extension speaker for a scanner.

Headphones

Headphones can be attached to most scanners by plugging them into the external loudspeaker socket. They are useful where other people don't want to be disturbed by the scanner's reception.

Choice of headphones is enormous but, personally, I prefer using a pair of lightweight ones sold for use with 'Walkman' type cassette players. They are very light, very comfortable and allow you to monitor and, at the same time hear the TV, for example. This type of headphone can be bought from most radio and hi-fi dealers for just a few pounds — do not buy expensive headphones, however, as their hi-fi qualities will be wasted on a scanner. One thing you will have to do before use is to change the plug. They are invariably fitted with a miniature three-pole jack plug and a two-pole plug is standard for connection to scanners. The lead into the headphone's jack plug will probably consist of two coaxial cables. The screens from both of these should be twisted together and soldered to the body (sleeve) connector of the replacement jack plug. The two inner cores should also be joined together and then soldered to the centre (tip) connector of the plug. Make sure that no short circuits between tip and body occur. This type of connection is called 'parallel' and, because these mini-headphones all are of high impedance, this method of connection will not harm the scanner. Other types of headphones, of low impedance, may damage the scanner if connected this way, however. Although the lightweight headphones

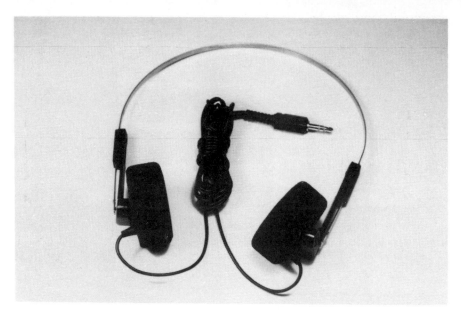

Photograph 6(b) Cheap personal stereo headsets are very light and comfortable and allow scanner listening without disturbing others. The three pole plug will have to be changed for a two pole miniature jack.

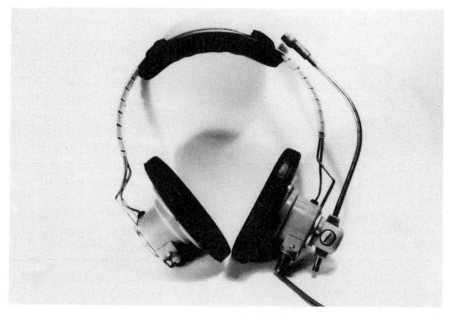

Photograph 6(c) A proper communication headset. These Airlite-62's are available for a few pounds from many government surplus dealers and once cleaned-up are ideal for scanner use. The microphone boom can easily be removed if not required.

mentioned here can be worn for hours without discomfort they do not exclude external noise. If noise exclusion is needed then heavier headphones of the type with ear muffs will have to be used. Again, the types stocked by hi-fi shops will do the job or you can get purpose made communication types from specialist dealers.

When buying any kind of headphone try them on in the shop. Some people find certain types of headphones very uncomfortable and they are very much a matter of personal choice.

Computer interfacing

In several chapters of this book reference has been made to connecting a scanner to a computer in order to interpret or decode certain types of transmission. Quite a large selection of computer software exists to do tasks like these for most of the major home computers, typically the Commodore 64 & VIC-20, BBC, Sinclair Spectrum & ZX-81, Dragon 32 & 64, Acorn Electron and some Amstrad models.

Interfaces

In most instances it is not possible to connect the audio output of the scanner straight into the computer. Under these circumstances it is necessary to use an interface. Interfaces vary in complexity from single transistor circuits to highly complex units capable of breaking down such things as transmitted satellite weather pictures into a digital form a computer can deal with.

On the other hand, there are cases where it *is* possible to connect the scanner directly to the computer. A typical example is the radioteletype (RTTY) program for my own Dragon 64 computer. Here the output from the scanner's loudspeaker socket is connected directly to the computer's cassette input port. Similar set-ups are available for other computers. This kind of arrangement, unfortunately only works with a strong clear signal. One of the advantages of using a proper interface is that it contains circuits to remove interference, cope with fading signals and so forth.

Let us now take a detailed look at the kind of software needed to decode various signals and the interfaces needed.

Morse code (CW)

Morse code decoding programs are available for most of home computers including the unexpanded ZX-81. Software available for Sinclair computers generally needs no interface. Other computers may need a simple single transistor tone decoder. Unfortunately there appears to be few of these decoders available as ready made units. Scarab Systems, however, can supply a simple unit for most home computers.

It is worth noting that most of the more complex RTTY decoders also work extremely well as CW decoders. The scanner, however, must have a BFO circuit and be capable of receiving CW.

Radioteletype (RTTY)

Often nicknamed the 'long distance typewriter' at VHF/UHF frequencies, RTTY transmissions are mostly found on amateur bands. Again, software and a computer can be used to print out the received and decoded transmissions. Much RTTY traffic is transmitted as an SSB signal which, can only be decoded if the scanner has suitable BFO circuitry. Some RTTY, though, is transmitted as dual-tone FM and to a lesser extent as AM. Software is available for a wide range of computers but in many cases a suitable decoder will be required and these are quite expensive.

Slow scan television (SSTV)

SSTV is a specialised type of transmission and is really only used to any great extent by amateurs. This means that the range of software available to decode SSTV transmissions for computer use is restricted but does exist. Some computers, such as the Sinclair Spectrum can be programmed with software that requires no interface. Most computers, however, require some kind of interface. Some RTTY decoders can also successfully be used to decode SSTV transmissions.

The quality of picture received depends largely on the screen resolution of the computer. Some older models only give a very coarse image but others such as the BBC and Commodore 64 provide excellent reproduction possibilities. With the right software, the received image may be dumped to a printer.

SSTV activity is found on the amateur VHF 2 metre band and the UHF 70 cm band. Look at the data in Chapter 7 for details. Unlike CW and RTTY, SSTV does not need a BFO circuit and can be received on any scanner capable of covering the bands. It can be recognised as a buzzing noise interspersed with blips of tone.

During 1985, amateurs around the world were thrilled to see SSTV pictures sent from the American space shuttle. On board the shuttle was an astronaut who holds an amateur radio licence and he was able to send back still pictures from several of the on-board cameras. I received pictures myself, using a Bearcat 220FB attached to a simple whip aerial in the garden. I recorded the tones that made up the pictures on an ordinary cassette recorder, later playing them back, via an interface, into a computer.

Availability of software

Table 6.1 is a list of available software which has been compiled from advertisements appearing in UK amateur radio magazines at the time of

Table 6.1 Available computer software to decode specialised transmissions

Computer	CW	RTTY	SSTV	Multi
ZX-81	●	●		
Spectrum	●	●	●	●
Commodore 64	●	●	●	●
VIC 20	●	●	●	●
Commodore 4/16/28	●	●		
BBC-B	●	●	●	●
Dragon 32/64	●	●		●
Amstrad CPC 464	●	●	●	
Atari 6/800XL	●			
Pet		●		

writing. A copy of any of the major magazines will enable a scanner user to find suitable software for an attached computer.

Multi means single programs able to cope with a variety of transmission types. Software is available in a variety of mediums including: cassette tape, disc, Sinclair Microdrive, plug-in cartridge and EPROM chip (BBC-B).

For details of suitable interface terminals see the equipment review on accessories in Chapter 9.

Weather pictures

Weather picture decoding is yet another application for computers hooked up to a scanner. So far, though, the only commercially available systems are for the BBC-B. Maplin and Halbar produce software.

Weather pictures are sent in a similar way to slow scan television in that the satellite's camera pictures are encoded into tones. These not only represent the various shades that make up the picture but also such things as syncronising pulses. For weather satellite transmission reception, the scanner must have a minimum of 30 kHz bandwidth in FM mode (WFM). Scanners such as the AOR's, Regency MX series, Yaesu and Icom are all capable of this.

Software for the BBC-B is on sideways-ROM or on disc.

The systems are designed to work primarily with NOAAs 8 and 9 satellites. These are polar orbiting satellites which make passes at about every 102 minutes, during which time the earth will turn through 25.5 degrees. The signals can be recorded on an ordinary cassette tape

Figure 6.1 A screen dump using the Computer Concepts 'Printmaster' ROM.

recorder and the Timestep interface has a circuit which will switch on the recorder when it detects a satellite signal. In this way it is possible to leave the equipment alone and then play back the pictures later. These can be shown on the monitor screen or dumped to a dot-matrix printer (see Figure 6.1).

Facilities are available on some interfaces to decode signals from other satellites, notably those of Russian origin and some can even be configured for normal slow scan television.

Frequencies of various satellite transmissions are given in Chapter 7.

Frequency converters

Frequency converters are devices that can be used with scanners to increase the frequency coverage. They fall into two categories; simple general-purpose types and dedicated systems. Frequency converters of the first category can be used with virtually any scanner whereas those of the second work only with particular scanners. The converters, while capable of filling in frequency gaps on some scanners or extending their upper range, have a restriction in that when they are in use, reception on the scanner's other frequency ranges is not possible.

Several converters are available in the UK and typical is the Samtron U-Verter. It comprises a box of circuitry with an aerial socket, output socket and 12 volt supply line. The output of the converter is connected to the scanner's aerial input. In use, it is a matter of looking up a table on the front of the converter which tells you which VHF frequency to enter into the scanner to receive transmissions on the required UHF frequency.

Other converters working on a similar principle are a UHF down-converter and HF up-converter, both sold by A.R.E. Communications. The first provides coverage from 800 MHz to 1.5 SHz or higher depending on the scanner used. The second provides coverage from 1—30 MHz

SX-400 system

The only other available frequency converters are the dedicated SX-400 modules. They are designed to work with the JIL SX-400 scanner. There are two down-converters, the RF-8014 and the RF5080. The RF-8014 extends SX-400 coverage from 800 to 1400 MHz; the RF5080 from 500 to 800 MHz. When in use with the SX-400, the scanner sends a control signal to the converter, switching it into or out of circuit.

JIL also offers an up-converter for the SX-400 which operates in the same way. In this case, though, the converter covers the entire LF/MF/HF spectrum from 100 kHz to 30 MHz. This module also has extra facilities such as allowing reception of SSB and CW transmissions.

These converters will also work with some other scanners but will not automatically switch in and out of circuit.

Specifications of all converters are given in Chapter 9.

Miscellaneous

Aerial switch

There may be occasions when a scanner user needs to change aerials connected to the scanner. For instance, although a discone is suitable for reception of most transmissions, if the user wishes to receive satellite transmissions a crossed dipole is required. Obviously it is of no great hardship to unplug one aerial and plug in the other, but a neater solution is an aerial switch. These usually consist of a small box with a switch of rotary, toggle or push button type. In use the two aerial connections form inputs to the switch box and the output, after switching, is fed to the scanner. They vary greatly in quality and some of the cheaper types, particularly those sold as CB accessories, may have enormous losses at VHF/UHF frequencies. If you wish to use an aerial switch: make sure it is of the right type to match your scanner and aerial systems.

Slide mount bracket

One problem with using a scanner in a vehicle is that the equipment is at the mercy of thieves. One answer to this is to use a quick-release slide mounting bracket which allows the scanner to be easily removed — by the owner! They are widely available from CB radio dealers and consist of two parts: a holder and a sliding carrier. The holder is fitted with contacts that match up to contacts on the sliding section. The contacts are used to allow plug-in connections for power supply and external loudspeaker purposes, to and from the scanner.

Some users also use contacts for the aerial feed but this is not a good ideal as the type of contacts used are not suited to low-level radio signals.

Installation of a slide mount bracket is fairly straightforward, but a soldering iron will be needed to make connections to the contacts. The scanner itself is bolted to the slide carrier. The holder is located in a suitable position; fixed with either self-tapping screws or small nuts and bolts.

In use, the sliding carrier complete with scanner is quickly removed, and while the owner is away from the vehicle, can be stored, say, in the boot, where it is out of temptation's way.

UK frequency allocations 7

The decision on who transmits what, on which frequency, is made by international agreement. Clearly, governments must agree on allocations if they are to avoid causing interference. There would be chaos if, say, one country allocated a band to low powered radio telephones while a neighbouring country allocated the same band for high powered broadcasting. The body which co-ordinates radio frequency allocations on behalf of world governments is the International Telecommunications Union, known simply as the ITU.

For the purpose of agreed allocations the ITU splits the world into three regions. The United Kingdom falls in Region 1, which includes most of Europe and a small section of North Africa. However, it does not necessarily follow that each country conforms strictly with the allocations drawn up for that region. Where there is little likelihood of interference, countries may opt for local variations and, obviously, many such variations exist. For this reason, listings given in this book strictly apply only to the United Kingdom, although most allocations do match the standard format for Region 1.

We shall look first at general VHF/UHF frequency allocations, then consider in detail some of the services on those allocations. Table 7.1 is a listing of UK VHF frequency allocations and Table 7.2 is a similar listing of UK UHF frequency allocations.

Table 7.1 UK VHF frequency allocations

Frequency band (MHz)	Allocated services
27.500—27.600	Met — LandM —Pagers
27.600—28.000	Met — CB (channellised)
28.000—29.700	Amateur
29.700—30.005	LandM (Gov)

Table 7.1 *continued*

Frequency band (MHz)	Allocated services
30.005—30.010	Space (sat ident)
30.010—31.700	LandM (Gov)
31.700—31.725	Fix — mobile
31.725—31.775	Pagers (hospital)
31.775—35.925	Fix — mobile
34.925—34.975	Emergency alarms
34.975—35.005	Fix — mobile
35.005—35.205	Model control
35.205—37.500	Mobile
37.500—38.250	Mobile — astro
38.250—40.660	Mobile
40.050	*Military distress fcy
40.660—40.700	ISM
40.700—47.440	LandM
47.440—47.550	Cordless 'phones
47.550—50.000	LandM
50.000—50.500	Amateur
50.500—68.000	LandM
68.000—70.050	LandM (Gov)
70.025—70.500	Amateur
70.500—71.500	LandM (emgcy)
71.500—72.800	LandM (PMR)
72.800—74.800	LandM (Gov+PMR)
74.800—75.200	Aero navigation
75.200—76.700	LandM (Gov+PMR)
76.700—78.000	Fix — LandM — MarM
78.000—80.000	LandM
80.000—84.000	Fix — LandM — Astro
84.000—85.000	Fix — LandM (Gov)
85.000—88.000	Fix — LandM (PMR)
88.000—97.600	Broadcast
97.600—102.100	LandM (emgcy)
102.100—107.790	Broadcast
107.790—108.000	Emergency alarms
108.000—117.800	Aero navigation
118.000—136.000	Aero mobile (channellised)
121.500	*Aero distress
123.100	*Aero search and rescue
136.000—138.00	Space (weather sats)

Table 7.1 *continued*

Frequency band (MHz)	Allocated services
138.000—141.000	LandM (PMR)
141.000—141.900	LandM — space
141.900—143.000	LandM (Gov) — space
143.000—144.000	LandM (emgcy)
144.000—146.000	Amateur
146.000—149.000	LandM (emgcy)
149.000—150.050	Satellite navigation
150.050—152.000	Astro — slick markers
152.000—153.000	LandM (emgcy)
153.000—153.500	LandM — met
153.025—153.475	Wide area paging
154.000—156.000	LandM (emgcy)
156.000	*Lifeboat/coastguard
156.025—157.450	Marine mobile
156.375	*Coastguard rescue
156.800	*Marine distress
157.450—158.400	Message handling
158.400—158.530	Fixed — mobile
158.530—160.000	Carphone (vehicle)
159.930—160.625	Message handling
160.625—161.000	Marine mobile
161.000—161.120	Paging (+ acknowledge)
161.120—161.500	Fix — mobile
161.500—162.025	Marine mobile
162.025—163.030	Message handling
163.030—164.450	Carphone (base)
164.450—165.040	Message handling
165.040—173.200	Fix — LandM — ISM
173.200—173.350	Telemetry — telecontrol
173.350—174.414	Deaf aids
173.700—174.000	Medical
173.800—175.020	Radio microphones
174.000—225.000	Fix — LandM — locators
225.000—273.000	Fix — LandM (Gov)
235.000—273.000	Mobile satellite service
243.000	*Mil aero distress — SARBEs
273.000—300.000	Fix — LandM (Gov) — astro

Table 7.2 UK UHF frequency allocations

Frequency band (MHz)	Allocated services
300.00—328.60	Fix — mobile (Gov)
326.50—328.50	Astro (Jodrell Bank)
328.60—335.40	Aero navigation (ILS)
335.40—399.90	Fix — mobile (Gov)
399.90—400.05	Satellite navigation
400.05—400.15	Standard frequency
400.15—401.00	Met
401.00—402.00	Space (space — earth)
401.00—403.00	Weather satellites
401.00—405.00	Fix (Gov)
401.00—406.00	Mobile (Gov)
406.00—406.10	Space (space — earth)
406.10—410.00	Fix — mobile (Gov) — astro
406.50—409.50	Positioning aids
410.00—420.00	Fix — mobile (Gov)
420.00—450.00	Fix — mobile — loc (Gov)
432.00—440.00	Amateur
450.00—454.00	Fix — mobile
454.00—455.00	Wide area paging
455.00—457.50	Fix — mobile
457.50—458.50	Fix (point-to-point)
458.50—459.00	Model control
459.10—459.50	Paging (+ acknowledge)
459.50—470.00	Fix — mobile (PMR)
470.00—582.00	Television
582.00—606.00	Aero navigation
606.00—854.00	Television — fixed — astro
854.00—862.00	Fix — LandM
862.00—864.00	LandM (emgcy)
864.00—870.00	Mobile (not aero)
870.00—889.00	Fix — mobile (Gov)
886.00—906.00	ISM
888.00—889.00	Anti-theft devices
889.00—890.00	Mobile (emgcy)
890.00—905.00	Mobile (cellular radio)
905.00—934.00	Mobile — radiolocation (Gov)
934.00—935.00	Citizens' band (CB)
935.00—960.00	Mobile (cellular radio)
960.00—1215.00	Aero navigation

Table 7.2 *continued*

Frequency band (MHz)	Allocated services
1215.00—1240.00	Radiolocation (Gov) — space
1215.00—1365.00	Civil airfield radar
1240.00—1325.00	Amateur
1260.00—1300.00	Radiolocation (Gov)

There follows a glossary of abbreviations and definitions used in Tables 7.1 and 7.2.

Aero distress Frequencies allocated for distress use only.

Aero mobile Aeronautical mobile is assigned for communications between aircraft and ground installations. The main international band lies between 118—136 MHz.

Aero navigation Radio devices for navigating aircraft. They include VHF omni-range (VOR), doppler VOR (DVOR), distance measuring equipment (DME), instrument landing system (ILS), tactical navigation (TACAN), fan marker (MM), etc.

Aero search and rescue Frequencies allocated solely for use by aircraft involved in search and rescue.

Amateur The amateur service is for use by licensed individuals to pursue radio communication for experimenting and self-training.

Astro Frequencies assigned for radio astronomy.

Broadcast General transmissions for reception by the public. May be sound or television.

Carphone A communication system fitted to a vehicle which communicates with a base station connected to the public telephone exchange.

CB Citizens' band. Low powered communications service available to the public.

Cellular A more sophisticated version of the carphone.

Cordless phone A telephone handset that does not require direct connection to the exchange line.

Emgcy Emergency. Allocations for police, fire and ambulance services.

Fix Fixed station. A base station that is linked via radio to another base station, as opposed to mobiles. Often referred to as point-to-point.

ISM Industrial, scientific and medical. The ISM allocations are for equipment that relies on the emission of radio waves but not for communication purposes.

LandM Land mobile. Communication between a fixed base and mobile or portable equipment.

Loc Locator. The transmission of radio signals for navigation, positioning and tracking.

MarM Maritime mobile. Services for ship-to-shore and ship-to-ship communication.

Met Equipment used for meteorological observation and measuring.

Mobile Any mobile service. Air, marine or land.

Mobile satellite service Allocated for communication between a mobile station and a space satellite.

Model control The use of radio signals to control the movement of model aircraft, boats, cars, etc.

Message handling Similar to PMR but many individual mobile stations working through a central base station.

On-site paging A paging service designed solely for use in a restricted area.

Pager A small radio receiver designed to emit a warning that a pre-coded signal has been received.

Positioning aid A beacon that is used to emit a radio signal for navigation purposes. Often used at sea to position such vessels as oil rigs.

PMR Private mobile radio. Allocations available to non-government organisations for communication between a base station and mobiles.

Radio microphone A microphone used in broadcast studios and theatres. It transmits its output as a low powered radio signal which is picked up by a receiver and amplified.

SARBE Search and rescue beacon. A small radio transmitter attached to a lifejacket or dinghy.

Satellite navigation Position fixing by reference to orbiting satellites.

Slick marker A low powered floating beacon that is used to check the movement of oil slicks.

Standard frequency Transmission of a highly stable signal which can be used as a frequency reference. Normally the transmission includes coded signals of accurate time.

Space Frequency assigned for earth-space operations.

Telemetry A radio signal containing data in coded form.

Telecontrol A signal containing command information to control remote equipment.

Television A radio signal containing information relating to visual images.

Weather satellite A space satellite that sends weather pictures back to an earth station.

Wide area paging A paging service not confined to a private site.

In addition there is mention of some low powered radio transmitting devices: deaf aids, emergency signalling devices and anti-theft devices.

Aeronautical bands

Aeronautical and marine bands, unlike all other bands, are standard world wide. Aircraft transmissions are of two kinds: civilian and military.

Civilian aircraft transmissions use two bands: HF using SSB for long distance communication, and VHF for communications up to distances of several hundred miles. All communications (civilian and military) are amplitude modulated.

Civilian airport transmissions

A list of UK civilian airports and corresponding transmission frequencies is given in Table 7.3. These are believed to be current frequencies but it should be noted that they are occasionally changed.

Table 7.3 British and Irish civilian airports and ground stations

	Approach Depart	Tower	Frequencies MHz/AM mode Homer	Radar or LARS	Ground	AT/AFIS or misc
Aberdeen	120.40	118.10	121.25	128.30	121.70	121.85
Alderney (CI)	128.65	123.60				
Andrewsfield Radio						130.55
Bantry (EI)						122.40
Barrow (Walney)		123.20				
Beccles	134.60	122.95				
Belfast (Aldergrove)	120.00	118.30	120.90			
	353.80	353.80		243.00		
Belfast (Harbour)	130.85	130.75	130.85	122.45		
Belmullet						123.60
Bembridge Radio						123.25
Benbecula	119.20	119.20				119.20
Biggin Hill	129.40	134.80				
Birmingham	120.50	118.30	120.50	120.50	121.80	112.90
Blackbushe						122.30
Blackpool	118.40	118.40	118.40	119.95		
Bourn						129.80
Bournemouth (Hurn)	118.65	125.60		119.75		
Bridlington Radio						123.25
Bristol (Lulsgate)	127.75	120.55	127.75	124.35		127.60
Brough						130.85
Caernafon Radio						122.25
Cambridge	123.60	122.20	123.60	130.75		
	294.60			294.60		
Cardiff	125.85	121.20	125.85	120.05		
Carlisle	123.60	123.60				
Carnmore (EI)						122.50
Castlebar (EI)						122.60

Table 7.3 *continued*

	Approach Depart	Tower	*Frequencies MHz/AM mode* Homer	Radar or LARS	Ground	AT/AFIS or misc
Castlebridge (EI)						123.00
Chichester	122.45	119.70				
Compton Abbas						122.70
Cork (EI)	119.90	119.30			121.80	121.70
Coventry	119.25	119.25	122.00	122.00		
Cranfield	122.85	123.20	122.85	122.85		
Denham Radio						130.725
Doncaster Radio						122.90
Dounray Thurso	122.40	122.40				
Dublin (EI)	121.10	118.60		119.55	121.80	118.50
Dundalk (EI)						122.90
Dundee	122.90	122.90				
Dunsfold	122.55	130.00	122.55	122.55		
	277.60	289.60	130.00	277.60		
Duxford						123.50
Earls Colne Radar				122.425		
East Midlands	119.65	124.00	119.65	124.00		
Edinburgh	121.20	118.70	121.20	121.20	121.75	124.25
Elstree Radio						122.40
Eniskillen						123.20
Enstone						129.875
Exeter	128.15	119.80	128.15	128.15		119.05
Fairoaks (AFIS)						123.425
Farranfore (EI)						122.60
Fenland (AFIS)						123.05
Fethard						123.30
Flotta						122.15
Gamston						130.475
Glasgow	119.10	118.80		119.30	121.70	113.40
Gloucester	125.65	125.65		122.90		
Great Yarmouth				123.45		120.45
Guernsey (CI)	128.65	119.95	124.50	118.90		109.40
Halfpenny Green						123.00
Hatfield	123.35	130.80		119.30		
	369.30	363.50		369.30		
Hawarden	123.35	124.95	123.35	129.85		
Headfort (EI)						123.30
Humberside	123.15	118.55	123.15			
Inishmore						123.30
Inverness	122.60	122.60				
Ipswich Radio						123.25
Isle of Man	120.85	118.90	120.85	118.20		125.30
Isle of Wight						123.50
Jersey (CI)	120.30	119.45			121.90	112.20
Kirkwall	118.30	118.30				
Lashenden Radio						122.00
Leavesden	122.15	122.15	122.15	121.40		

Table 7.3 *continued*

	Approach Depart	Tower	Frequencies MHz/AM mode Homer	Radar or LARS	Ground	AT/AFIS or misc
Leeds/Bradford	123.75	120.30	123.75	121.05		
Leicester Radio						122.25
Lerwick Tingwall						122.60
Little Snoring						122.40
Liverpool	119.85	118.10		118.45		
London City	132.7	119.425		128.025		121.775
London Gatwick	119.60	124.225		119.60	121.80	117.90
		127.55		118.95	121.95	121.75
London Heathrow	119.20	118.70		119.20	121.90	121.85
	120.40	121.00		119.50	121.70	115.10
	119.50	118.50		127.55		112.30
	127.55			120.40		133.075
	Helicopters & VFR			119.90		
London Stansted	126.95	118.15	126.95	125.55		123.80
				126.95		
London (Heliport)		122.90				
Londonderry	122.85	122.85				
Luton	129.55	120.20	129.55	128.75		
	128.75	121.75	127.30	127.30		
	127.30	398.00	128.75			
Lydd	120.70	120.70		131.30		
Manchester (Intnl)	119.40	118.70		119.40		128.175
	121.35	121.70		121.35		
Manchester (Barton)						122.70
Netherthorpe Radio						123.50
Newcastle	126.35	119.70	118.50	126.35		
	397.10					
Newtownards Radio						123.50
Northampton Sywell						122.60
Norwich	119.35	118.90	119.35	124.25		
Nottingham Radio						122.80
Oxford (Kidlington)	130.20	119.80				
Pailton Test						126.05
Panshanger Info						120.25
Paull Radio						123.00
Penzance Heliport						118.10
Perth (Scone)	122.30	119.80	122.30			
Peterborough (Con)						123.00
Peterborough (Sib)						122.30
Plymouth	123.20	122.60				
Popham Radio						129.80
Preston	122.55	130.80				
Prestwick	120.55	118.15		119.60		
Redhill (AFIS)						123.225
Rochester (AFIS)						122.25
Samlesbury	122.55	130.80				
Sandtoft Radio						130.425

Table 7.3 *continued*

| | Approach Depart | Tower | Frequencies MHz/AM mode | | | |
			Homer	Radar or LARS	Ground	AT/AFIS or misc
Saxa Vord						118.15
Scatsa	123.60	123.60		122.40		
Scilly Isles						123.15
Seething Radio						122.60
Shannon	121.40	118.70		121.40		121.70
	120.20	121.80				
Sherburn Radio						122.60
Shetland Radar				118.15		
Shobdon Radio						123.50
Sligo (EI)						122.10
Shoreham	123.15	125.40	123.15			
Southampton	128.85	118.20		131.00		121.30
Southend	128.95	119.70	128.95	129.45	125.05	
S. Marston (AFIS)						130.425
Strapleford (AFIS)						122.80
Stornoway (AFIS)						123.50
Strathallen Radio						123.50
Sturgate Radio						130.30
Sumburgh	123.15	118.25		123.15		125.85
	119.25			130.05		
Sunderland	122.20	122.70				
Swansea	119.70	119.70	119.70	120.75		
Teeside	118.85	119.80	128.85	118.85		
Thruxton Radio						130.45
Tiree						122.70
Viking Approach	129.95					
Warton	122.55	130.80	122.55			
Waterford						129.85
Weston (EI)						122.40
Weston	129.25	122.50				
White Waltham						122.60
Wick	119.70	119.70				
Wickenby Radio						122.45
Woodford	130.05	122.50		130.75		
Wycombe Air Park						126.55
Yeovil	130.80	125.40		130.80		
	364.30	294.60		226.00		

If an aerial is used solely for airband reception then it should be vertically polarised. It is worth noting, by the way, that a simple ground plane aerial of the type described in Chapter 5 is more than adequate for aircraft band-only operation.

What you might hear
Remember that aircraft transmissions are usually short and there may be long periods when nothing is heard on a frequency. This applies, in

particular, to smaller airfields where traffic movement may be quite low.

In addition to approach, control tower and radar landing instructions you may also hear a variety of other messages being passed on other frequencies in the bands. Many airlines have 'company frequencies' on which aircraft crews and ground operation staff communicate. You may also hear transmissions relating to zone, area or sector controllers. These are the people who control the movements of aircraft as they fly between airports. Different sectors have different transmission frequencies and so, to follow a particular aircraft as it moves from one sector to another, you will need to change your reception frequencies, to suit.

At London Heathrow and similar large airports, the sheer volume of traffic means that instructions passed to the aircraft must be done by several controllers and so you may come across frequencies which are dealing solely with such things as instructions on taxiing on the ground.

Continuous transmissions

Some frequencies are allocated solely for transmissions from the ground. The aircraft never transmit on these frequencies but the crews may listen to the broadcasts for information. The most common of these are 'VOLMETS', transmitted round the clock and detailing current weather conditions for most major airports.

Automatic terminal information service (ATIS) transmissions, on the other hand, are sent out by individual airports and only include details of that airport, including current weather, runway and approach patterns in use, and any other essential information. They, in fact, contain all the information a pilot needs except actual landing permission. Pilots will listen to these transmissions and when contacting the controller will often be heard to say such things as 'information Bravo received'. The word 'Bravo' standing for the code letter which identifies the start of an ATIS transmission. ATIS transmissions are made in the navigation aid band (108–118 MHz).

Range

As we mentioned earlier in the book, range is difficult to define as it is affected by so many factors. Using a reasonable outside aerial it may be possible to hear ground stations up to 20 miles or so away. However, if hills or large buildings are between the scanner and the airport then this range will be considerably reduced. For instance, in my own case I cannot pick up my local airport which is only four miles away and yet can pick up another airport which is some 25 miles away in a different direction.

Air-to-ground range though is a different matter altogether. Aircraft flying at tens of thousands of feet may be heard several hundred miles away even though the scanner is only operating on a small telescopic aerial. This is because the line-of-site range is greatly extended by the height of the aircraft which is transmitting from a point where there are no obstructions to block or weaken the signal.

You will hear many unfamiliar expressions and considerable use of abbreviations in the airband. If you are not familiar with these, you can look them up in the airband section in Chapter 8.

Notes on civilian airport frequencies
Occasionally frequencies may be interchanged and, for instance, approach control will be handled by the tower. However, all the airfields shown do have their main frequencies listed. Ground handling frequencies, where they are used, have not been included as it is easy to pick these up when the tower hands over the aircraft and instructs the pilot on which frequency to change to.

Military airport transmissions

Military airport transmissions use the same frequencies as civilian airports, but also have frequency allocations between 240 and 350 MHz. A list of UK military airports and corresponding transmission frequencies is given in Table 7.4.

Table 7.4 Main military air allocations

Airfield	LOC	MATZ	Appr'ch	Tower	PAR	SRE	VDF	Misc
Aberporth (MOD)	EGUC	122.150						353.850
Abingdon	EGUD	120.900	299.100	130.250		123.300		
				256.500		259.300		
Barkston Heath	EGYE	119.000	307.700	367.200				
Bedford (Thurleigh)	EGVW	124.400	130.700	130.000	118.350	124.400	277.250	
			287.100	241.350	356.700	277.250		
Benson	EGUB	120.900	299.100	398.700		123.300	299.100	314.400
			362.300	122.100		359.300	259.300	
Bentwaters (USAF)	EGVJ	119.000	308.500	292.850	308.500	119.000		356.000
Binbrook	EGXB	125.350	383.900	242.650	256.050	362.300	256.050	257.800
Boscombe Down	EGDM	126.700	264.500	130.000	130.750	313.200	264.500	370.850
		264.520		242.200	290.550	340.000	126.700	289.800
Boulmer Rescue	EGOM	123.100	285.850	233.700	282.800			
Brawdy	EGDA	124.400	292.000	243.300	123.300	276.300		
			362.300	257.800	387.350	313.200		
			341.050	122.100	353.900	123.300		
Bristol Filton	EGTG	130.850	244.700	124.950		132.350		290.350
Brize Norton	EGVN	119.000	133.750	126.500	134.300	133.750	134.300	363.500
			246.550	249.750	308.750	359.100	308.750	288.850
			292.400	257.800		341.300	246.450	252.350

Table 7.4 *continued*

Airfield	LOC	MATZ	Appr'ch	Tower	PAR	SRE	VDF	Misc
Chivenor	EGDC	130.200 315.450	309.900 122.100	318.150 286.950	123.300 227.200	381.400 387.650	309.900 315.450	381.400
Church Fenton	EGXG	126.500	381.800 362.300	359.800 257.800	123.300 356.700	231.000 362.300		385.400
Coltishall	EGYC	125.900	379.200 387.850	142.290 288.850	123.300 371.000	361.650	379.200	284.575 275.450
Coningsby	EGXC	120.800 370.900	362.300 345.150	120.800 234.950	342.600 358.100	276.650 344.000		318.150 123.300
Cosford	EGWC		234.100	292.100				122.100
Cottesmore	EGXJ	130.200 266.050	354.400 234.850	130.200 246.400	297.600 370.450	266.050 317.700		123.300 122.100
Cranfield	EGTC	372.100	122.850 341.800	123.200		122.850		
Cranwell	EGYD	119.000	297.900 362.300	380.100 257.800		364.500 344.000		122.100 123.300
Croughton (USAF)	EG							353.600
Culdrose	EGDR	134.050	292.700	289.100 130.400	246.300 123.300	134.050		305.600 310.200
Dishforth	EGXD							
Dunsfold	EGTD		122.550 241.800	124.325 287.500		118.825	124.325	
Fairford (USAF)	EGVA	119.000	246.450 362.300	119.150 380.000				276.550 257.800
Falmouth Radar	EG					134.050		326.000
Farnborough	EGUF	130.050	134.350 296.250	122.500 387.600	130.050 353.850	125.250 296.250	275.550 296.250	359.700
Finningly	EGXI	120.350 293.700	398.500	315.700 122.100	123.300 371.800	293.700 368.400		276.000 344.000
Greenham Common	EGVI			266.800 358.350		257.500		276.550 122.100
Haverfordwest	EGFE	124.400						122.200
Honington	EGXH	129.050 361.600	355.350 362.300	233.850 257.800	241.550 385.400	226.350 344.000		318.150 123.300
Kemble	EGDK	363.100	362.300 123.300	335.550 122.100		293.800 363.950		122.100
Kinloss	EGQK	119.350 394.100	319.000 362.300	287.000 257.800	288.450 387.850	352.500 123.300		
Lakenheath (USAF)	EGUL	129.050	379.800 243.600	231.500 257.800	148.400 300.350	309.000 344.000		248.450 355.700
Leconfield Rescue	EGXV	122.100	297.800	282.800				

Table 7.4 *continued*

Airfield	LOC	MATZ	Appr'ch	Tower	PAR	SRE	VDF	Misc
Leeming Radar	EGXE					132.400 286.000	359.200 362.300	122.100
Lee-on-Solent	EGUS			135.700				340.500
Leuchars	EGQL	126.500	257.700 362.300	269.000 122.100	318.900 353.850	288.300 123.300	126.500	120.800 290.700
Linton-on-Ouse	EGXU	129.150	357.500 362.300	246.800 257.800	335.700 288.100	361.200 344.000		398.300 122.100
Llanbedr	EGOD	122.500	288.450	294.600	365.900		365.900	
London Mil Radar	EGWD	250.600	342.800					
Lossiemouth	EGQS	119.350 394.100	319.000 362.300	118.900 291.000	288.750 286.550	352.500 387.350	318.500 319.000	355.250 259.400
Lyneham	EGDL		118.425 315.750	123.400 293.100	360.650 383.400	276.350 344.000	123.400	318.950 362.300
Machrihanish	EGQJ	125.900	287.050 362.300	285.600 257.800	354.200 385.400	289.600 344.000		122.100 123.300
Manston	EGUM		126.350 352.500	124.900 362.100	390.300 385.400	387.000 123.300	126.350 129.450	362.300
Marham	EGYM	124.150	265.800 362.300	275.350 257.800	317.950 385.400	340.750 344.000	124.150 122.100	123.300 318.750
Middle Wallop	EGVP	126.700	314.900	267.100	365.300	280.400		257.800
Mildenhall (USAF)	EGUN		129.050 355.350	122.550 250.000				297.400
Netheravon	EGDN		254.000	128.300				233.400
Newton	EGXN	122.100	227.500	360.300		362.300		257.800
Northolt	EGWU		134.150 362.300	275.650 257.800	130.350 244.550	355.400 130.350	377.500 134.150	257.800 129.125
Odiham	EGVO	125.250 318.100	341.000 362.300	378.550 257.800	364.050 385.400	275.550		269.700 122.100
Portland	EGDP	282.800	124.150 317.800	291.000 362.300	387.500	317.800 362.300		122.100 123.300
St. Athan	EGDX	122.100	230.300 362.300	352.900 257.800		352.400 277.600		385.400 344.000
St. Mawgan	EGDG	126.500	352.850 362.300	123.400 286.200	394.500 385.400	125.550 387.750	352.850 387.850	123.300 344.000
Salisbury Plain A/G	EG	130.150						253.500
Shawbury	EGOS	124.150	364.100 362.300	359.200 257.800	341.600 385.400	265.200 344.000		382.200 122.100
Shetland FIS	EGQR	285.650						
Topcliffe	EGXZ	132.400 286.000	125.000 382.600	293.100 257.800		290.800 385.400		122.100 362.300

Table 7.4 *UK continued*

Airfield	LOC	MATZ	Appr'ch	Tower	PAR	SRE	VDF	Misc
Upper Heyford	EGUA	128.550	316.850			362.300		
Valley	EGOV	134.350	378.900	307.400	319.000	352.500	122.100	387.500
			362.300	257.800	385.400	123.300	134.350	
Waddington	EGXW	127.350	247.900	383.600	309.100	258.850	127.350	122.100
			362.300	257.800	385.400	344.000		123.300
Warton	EGNO	124.450	286.750	130.800		286.750		
		352.800	254.350	254.350		254.350		
Wattisham	EGUW	123.400	299.200	353.500	355.050	300.250	299.200	122.100
			362.300	122.100	286.200	286.200	123.400	123.300
West Freugh (MOD)	EGOY	130.050	387.550	122.550		387.550		
			130.050	241.350		353.850		
Wethersfield (USAF)	EGVT	122.100						
Wittering Radar	EGXT	130.200	240.550			316.000		123.300
Woodbridge (USAF)	EGVG	119.000	255.800	119.150				307.400
				257.800				291.350
Woodford	EGCD	130.500	122.500	126.925		130.750		
			243.400	336.600		336.600		
Woodvale	EGOW		120.650	233.100				344.800
Wyton	EGUY	134.050	338.100	251.100	277.500	306.850		314.650
			362.300	257.800	385.400	265.750		225.600
Yeovilton	EGDY	127.350	276.700	310.200	340.400	353.300		265.700
		276.700	362.300	122.100	308.600	362.300		123.300
Common Frequencies in use at many fields			122.100	122.100		123.300		
			362.300	257.800		344.000		

In some instances, airports offer additional services such as precision approach radar (PAR) and surveillance radar element (SRE). In order to keep Table 7.4 sufficiently compact, these have been included under approach and tower headings.

The frequency 122.1 MHz is a standard tower frequency available at most military airports.

MATZ stands for 'military aerodrome traffic zone' and civilian aircraft are not allowed in these areas without permission. Calls to obtain permission will be made on the MATZ frequency shown.

As with the civilian listings, many of the frequencies are interchangeable and it is not unusual for, say, the MATZ frequency to also be used for approach control or radar services.

Miscellaneous airband services

In addition to general airport approach, take off and landing services, there are a wide variety of other services. Aircraft need to be passed from one region to another and their use of designated airways needs to be controlled. When an aircraft is approaching London, for instance, it will have to change frequencies several times as it is handed from one sector to another. Crossing the borders of different countries also means a change of frequency to a new ground controller. Following an aircraft is easy as it is standard procedure in airband communication for the ground controller to tell the pilot which frequency to change to and for the pilot to repeat the frequency he has been given.

Table 7.5 lists a selection of controller frequencies in the UK and Ireland.

Table 7.5 UK and Irish ground control transmission frequencies

Ground control	*Frequencies (MHz)*			
Border Radar (Boulmer)	132.900	134.850	233.700	
Eastern Radar (Watton)	128.425	135.200	288.500	
Falmouth Radar	134.050	326.000		
Jersey Zone	125.200	120.450		
London Control (VHF)	126.825	123.900	128.400	126.450
	128.500	125.950	128.900	126.300
	132.050			
London Control (UHF)	387.550	285.950	267.000	289.150
London Radar	119.200	119.900		
London (FIS)	124.750	124.600	132.600	131.050
	134.250			
London Military Radar	250.600	342.800		
Manchester Control	124.200	125.100	126.650	133.400
	119.400	121.350		
Midland Radar (N. Luffenham)	132.250	307.500		
Scottish Control (upper airspace)	135.850	124.050	124.500	
Scottish Control (FIS)	133.200	124.900	126.250	128.500
	131.300			
Shannon	131.150	135.600	132.150	124.700
	127.500	127.900		
Shanwick Oceanic	123.950	127.650	135.525	133.800

Emergency frequencies

Table 7.6 lists the allocated UK emergency frequencies and services.

In addition to being allocated for emergency communications use, frequencies 121.5 MHz and 243.0 MHz are also used for search and rescue beacons of three forms. The first is a small transmitter emitting a radio bleep. It is triggered automatically when a crash occurs, or may be

Table 7.6 UK emergency frequencies and services

Service	Frequency (MHz)
Civilian	121.5
Search and rescue	123.1
Military	243.0
Scene of search (Plymouth rescue centre)	244.6
NATO	282.8
Lifeboat/coastguard	156.0
Distress	156.8

switched on manually. The second type contains a voice transmitter. The third type also includes a receiver, so turning it into a full, two-way communications transceiver. These beacons are either hand-held or, in the case of SARBE versions, fitted to lifejackets.

The Plymouth rescue centre is the main co-ordinating centre for rescues involving the Royal Navy and Royal Air Force in the English Channel area.

Frequencies 156.0 MHz and 156.8 MHz (both marine frequencies) are used by search and rescue aircraft to communicate with lifeboats, etc.

Navigational aids
Between the frequencies 108 MHz and 117.95 MHz you will hear a variety of navigational aids. These are VHF omni-range beacons (VOR) and instrument landing systems (ILS). Some of these services are paired with navigational aids on other bands to give additional services such as distance measuring (DME). Combined VOR/DME services are called VORTACS — the TAC part being a shortening of TACAN which in turn stands for 'tactical navigation'.

Although it *is* possible to hear these beacons, lists have not been included as they are not of interest to scanner users. The signals consist of nothing more than a short sequence of letters transmitted over and over again in morse code.

Table 7.7 Main VOLMETS providing weather information

Service	Frequency (MHz)
London VOLMET main	135.375
London VOLMET north	126.600
London VOLMET south	128.600

VOLMETS
These are transmit-only stations providing constantly updated weather information for a variety of major airports. The main ones are listed in Table 7.7.

Marine band

This, like the VHF airband, is one of the few international bands; it is common to *all* ITU regions.

It is channelised in that radio equipment made for marine VHF use does not usually have facilities to tune to a given frequency, instead it has a channel selector which goes from channel 1 to channel 88. A list of marine band channels and their transmission frequencies is given in Table 7.8.

Channels are designated for specific uses in that some are for ship-to-shore use, others for ship-to-ship, and so forth. The method of operating on marine band is very different from airband. On marine bands there is a common calling frequency which is also the main distress frequency: channel 16, at 156.8 MHz. When a ship wishes to call a shore station, even though the operator may know the channel that is used by that shore station, he will still make first contact on channel 16. Once contact is made the ship and shore station will then move to a 'working channel' — in most instances this will be the station's 'prime' channel for general transmissions, or 'link' channel for link calls (ie, ship-to-shore telephone calls).

Channels 0 and 67 are exclusively by lifeboats and coast guard vessels. Some search and rescue aircraft also have the facility to work these channels.

Table 7.8 shows that many channels have two frequencies. This is to enable duplex operation. Because these *are* duplex transmissions, it is impossible for a scanner to simultaneously monitor both frequencies. Two scanners would have to be used, each tuned to one of the two frequencies, if the whole transmission was to be received.

Table 7.9 lists general marine services on the marine band together with channel used.

Range
The useful range for marine VHF communications tends to be somewhat better than for the same type of frequencies and power levels used across land. Quite simply, there are few obstructions at sea and maximum ranges of 50—100 miles are not unusual. However, while signals from a ship may be quite strong at a coastal station, the signals may deteriorate even a mile or two inland.

Table 7.8 Marine band channels together with corresponding transmission frequencies

Channel number	Frequency (MHz) Ship		Shore
0		156.000	
1	156.050		160.650
2	156.100		160.700
3	156.150		160.750
4	156.200		160.800
5	156.250		160.850
6		156.300	
7	156.350		160.950
8		156.400	
9		156.450	
10		156.500	
11		156.550	
12		156.600	
13		156.650	
14		156.700	
15		156.750	
16		156.800	
17		156.850	
18	156.900		161.500
19	156.950		161.550
20	157.000		161.600
21	157.050		161.650
22	157.100		161.700
23	157.150		161.750
24	157.200		161.800
25	157.250		161.850
26	157.300		161.900
27	157.350		161.950
28	157.400		162.000
60	156.025		160.625
61	156.075		160.675
62	156.125		160.725
63	156.175		160.775
64	156.225		160.825
65	156.275		160.875
66	156.325		160.925
67		156.375	

Table 7.8 *continued*

| Channel number | Frequency (MHz) | | |
	Ship		Shore
68		156.425	
69		156.475	
70		156.525	
71		156.575	
72		156.625	
73		156.675	
74		156.725	
77		156.875	
78	156.925		161.525
79	156.975		161.575
80	157.025		161.625
81	157.075		161.675
82	157.125		161.725
83	157.175		161.775
84	157.225		161.825
85	157.275		161.875
86	157.325		161.925
87	157.375		161.975
88	157.425		162.025
M		157.850	

Table 7.9 General marine services and channel allocations

Service	Channels
Ship-to-ship	6, 8, 9, 10, 13, 15, 17, 67, 68, 70, 72, 75, 76, 77, 78
Port operations (simplex)	9, 10, 11, 12, 13, 14, 15, 17, 67, 69, 71, 73, 74
Port operations (duplex)	1, 2, 3, 4, 5, 7, 18, 19, 20, 21, 22, 60, 61, 62, 63, 64, 65, 66, 78, 79, 80, 81, 82, 84
Public correspondence (link calls)	1, 2, 3, 4, 5, 7, 23, 24, 25, 26, 27, 28, 60, 61, 62, 63, 64, 65, 66, 82, 83, 84, 85, 86, 87, 88

Shore stations

Table 7.10 lists UK shore stations, together with their prime and link channels. All stations transmit local area navigation warnings (beacons out of action, hazardous floating objects, etc). Most, but not all, transmit local area weather forecasts and storm warnings.

Table 7.10 UK shore stations, prime and link channels

Station	Prime channel	Link channel
Anglesea	26	28/61
Bacton	07	63/64
Buchan	25	87
Cardigan Bay	27	84
Celtic	24	
Clyde	26	
Collafirth	24	
Cromarty	28	84
Cullercoats	26	
Forth	24	
Grimsby	27	04
Hastings	07	63
Hebrides	26	27
Humber	26	24/85
Ilfracombe	05	07
Islay	25	
Jersey (CI)	25/82	
Lands End	27	64/85/88
Lewis	05	
Malin Head	23	67/85
Morcambe Bay	04	82
Niton	04/28	81/85/24
N. Foreland	26	05/66
Orfordness	62	82
Orkney	26	
Pendennis	62	
Portpatrick	27	
Scillies	61	66
Severn	25	
Shetland	27	25
Skye	24	
Start Point	26	60/63
St Peter Port (CI)	12/78	
Stonehaven	26	
Thames	02	83
Whitby	25	28

Principal simplex allocations

Table 7.11 lists principal simplex services' allocated channels.

Table 7.11 Principal simplex services' channel allocations

Service	Channel
Calling and distress	16
Port operations (prime)	12
Port operations (alternative)	14
Small yacht safety	67
Marinas	M
Inter-ship (prime)	06
Inter-ship (alternative)	08

Amateur bands

Most general-purpose scanners will cover at least one of the VHF/UHF amateur bands. Although many scanner users may look to such things as air and marine bands as being the more exciting listening, amateur bands do have an attraction in that the operators are not subject to the same power restrictions, and so even at VHF and UHF amateur radio becomes international in its coverage. During the summer months, in particular, effects such as sporadic-E and tropospherical ducting can mean that signals can be picked up over several hundreds of miles.

British amateurs are restricted at VHF and UHF to 4 bands; 6 metre, 4 metre, 2 metre and 70 centimetre. There are other bands but these are beyond the coverage of most scanners.

6 metre band

The 6 metre band became available to British amateurs on the 1st of February 1985, on an allocation between 50.0 and 52.00 MHz.

Table 7.12 RSGB recommended frequency allocations

Frequency (MHz)	Allocation
50.000–50.100	CW and beacons only
50.100–50.500	Narrowband modes (SSB centred on 50.200)
50.500–51.000	All modes
51.000–51.100	Pacific DX window
51.100–52.000	All modes

This particular band is also available to amateurs in countries in Regions 2 and 3 (including the USA). There, the band lies between 50—54 MHz and many amateurs claim that because it is lower in frequency than 2 metre and 4 metre bands it should be possible at times to achieve very good distances. The Gibraltar beacon for example ZB2VHF, on 50.035 MHz, is regularly heard in Britain. Transatlantic communications have also been achieved, at these frequencies, in the past.

4 metre band

This band is one of the least used by amateurs, although the Amateur Radio Emergency Network, RAYNET, does favour it in some areas. Possibly one reason why it is not popular is that Britain is one of the few countries in the world with an allocation at these frequencies and so little if any international working is possible. The band extends from 70.025 to 70.5 MHz and the only allocations are as given in Table 7.13

Table 7.13 UK frequency allocations on the 4 metre band

Frequency (MHz)	Allocation
70.025—70.075	Beacons only
70.075—70.150	CW only
70.105—70.260	SSB and CW only
70.200	SSB calling frequency
70.260—70.400	All modes
70.260	Mobile calling frequency
70.300	RTTY calling frequency
70.350—70.400	Raynet
70.400—70.500	FM only
70.450	FM calling frequency

2 metre band

This is without a doubt the most popular amateur VHF band and signals can usually be heard on it in most areas at any time of day. The UK band extends from 144—146 MHz but in other regions the band is extended even higher. Equipment for this band is relatively cheap and portable which makes it a favourite with amateurs for local contact work..

Range on the band varies enormously. Varying conditions can mean that a transmission of several hundred watts output may only be heard 20 or 30 miles away at one time, while a signal of a few watts could be picked up hundreds of miles away at another time. Peak progagation

Table 7.14 UK frequency allocations on the 2 metre band

Block type	Frequency (MHz)	Allocation
	144.000	
	144.000–144.015	Moonbounce
CW only	144.050	CW calling
	144.100	CW ms reference
	144.150	
SSB/CW only	144.250	GB2RS slow CW
	144.260	Raynet
	144.300	SSB calling
	144.400	SSB ms reference
	144.500	
All modes	144.500	SSTV calling
	144.540	Forbidden use
	144.600	RTTY calling
	144.675	Data calling
	144.700	FAX calling
	144.750	ATV calling
	144.775	Raynet
	144.800	Raynet
	144.825	Raynet
	144.845	
Beacons only		
	144.990	
Repeater inputs	145.000	RO
	145.025	R1
	145.050	R2
	145.075	R3
	145.100	R4
	145.125	R5
	145.150	R6
	145.175	R7
	145.200	
FM Simplex	145.200	S8
channels	145.225	S9
	145.250	S10
	145.275	S11
	145.300	S12 RTTY/AFSK
	145.325	S13
	145.350	S14

Table 7.14 *continued*

Block type	Frequency (MHz)	Allocation
	145.375	S15
	145.400	S16
	145.425	S17
	145.450	S18
	145.475	S19
	145.500	S20 calling
	145.525	S21 GB2RS News
	145.550	S22 Talk-in
	145.575	S23
	─145.600─	
Repeater output	145.600	R0
	145.625	R1
	145.650	R2
	145.675	R3
	145.700	R4
	145.725	R5
	145.750	R6
	145.775	R7
	─145.800─	
Satellite working only		
	─146.000─	

tends to be in the summer when sporadic-E activity is at its highest. The band is used for a whole range of transmission types and several modes are used. Frequency allocation, listed in Table 7.4, is more by a sort of gentlemen's agreement than anything else. The band is organised into blocks of transmission types.

The abbreviation 'ms', used in Table 7.14, stands for 'meteor scatter', a method of bouncing a radio signal off the tail of a meteor or a meteor shower. A similar method of communication is involved in 'moon-bounce'. These types of communications are generally beyond the scope of scanner users as highly sensitive equipment and massive aerial arrays are required.

70 centimetre band

This band is allocated between 432.00 and 440 MHz. It is allocated on a 'secondary' basis which means that amateurs using it must not interfere with other services on the band. The other services are mainly navigational positioning beacons known as 'SYLEDIS'.

Table 7.15 UK frequency allocations on the 70 centimetre band

Block type	Frequency (MHz)	Allocation
	─432.000─	
CW only	432.000—432.015	Moonbounce
	432.050	CW calling
	─432.150─	
SSB/CW only	432.200	UK SSB calling
	432.300	IARU SSB calling
	─432.500─	
Modes	432.600	RTTY working
	432.600	RTTY calling
	432.675	Data calling
	432.700	FAX calling
	─432.800─	
Beacons		
	─433.000─	
Repeater outputs	433.000	RB0
	433.025	RB1
	433.050	RB2
	433.075	RB3
	433.100	RB4
	433.125	RB5
	433.150	RB6
	433.175	RB7
	433.200	RB8/SU8 Raynet
	433.225	RB9
	433.250	RB10
	433.275	RB11
	433.300	RB12/SU12+RTTY
	433.325	RB13
	433.350	RB14
	─433.375─	
FM simplex channels	433.375	SU15
	433.400	SU16
	433.425	SU17
	433.450	SU18
	433.475	SU19
	433.500	SU20 FM calling
	─434.600─	
Repeater outputs	434.600	RB0
	434.625	RB1

Table 7.15 *continued*

Block type	Frequency (MHz)	Allocation
	434.650	RB2
	434.675	RB3
	434.700	RB4
	434.725	RB5
	434.750	RB6
	434.775	RB7
	434.800	RB8
	434.825	RB9
	434.850	RB10
	434.875	RB11
	434.900	RB12+RTTY
	434.925	RB13
	434.950	RB14
	—435.000—	
	434.000—440.000	Devoted to amateur Fast Scan Television where there is no interference to other allocated users.
	435.000—438.000	Amateur satellite service.
	—440.000—	

The characteristics of the band are very similar to those of the 2 metre band with the exception that operators do not get the extreme ranges achieved at times on the 2 metre band. By and large the band is less used than the 2 metre band although in densely populated areas there can be a fairly high level of activity. As equipment for the band comes down in price, which it is doing, occupancy is likely to increase as many amateurs see the band as a means of escaping from the crowded 2 metre band.

Like the 2 metre band, the 70 centimetre band also has repeaters, throughout the country, which considerably increase the range of operation.

Frequency allocations, again divided into blocks of transmission types, is listed in Table 7.15.

Land mobile services

Under the banner of land mobile services is a varied range of communications users. In the following section you will find listed private mobile radio, emergency services, message handling and paging.

The term 'land mobile' applies to any radio communications that takes place between either mobile-to-mobile or mobile-to-base, across land as opposed to air or marine. The mobile can either be a vehicle installation or a portable transceiver of the walkie-talkie type.

Ranges of such equipment vary enormously. In open country ranges of 20 or 30 miles are not unusual but in built-up areas this may be cut to considerably less. Users of mobile radio equipment operating in towns and cities often use aerials on very high buildings well away from the actual point of operation. Connection between the operator and the remote aerial site is usually through a private telephone line. Emergency services may have even more sophisticated arrangements with several aerial/transmitter sites to give total coverage of an area. This becomes particularly important when communication is to and from low powered handsets with limited aerial facilities.

Private mobile radio (PMR)

Private mobile radio is a form of communication between a base station and one or more mobile or portable units. Typical examples are the transceivers used by taxi firms. PMR is not to be confused with the government allocations, emergency services or car radiophones, all of which fall into different categories and are listed elsewhere.

Communication in the PMR bands can be either FM or AM and may be split frequency, or single frequency simplex. Only one band, VHF band 3, is available for duplex working.

Table 7.16 shows all bands allocated to PMR communications, listing them with respect to frequency and service allocations.

Public radiophones

Radiophones, also known as carphones, form part of a radio communications system that is connected to the normal telephone exchange at the base station. It allows a telephone type handset to be installed in a vehicle capable of making or receiving telephone calls. The service only operates in major towns and cities. It has the disadvantage of limited range and is being replaced by a cellular radio telephone system which relies on a whole network of base stations. The 'cellphone' system is computer-controlled and as the vehicle moves out of range of one base station it is automatically switched to the frequency of the next closest cell. The VHF radiophone service is half-duplex but the UHF cellular service is fully duplex.

Both services are FM only and can handle data as well as voice communications. Table 7.17 lists the allocated frequencies of the VHF radiophone band, while Table 7.18 lists those of the UHF cellular band.

Table 7.16 UK private mobile radio bands and frequency allocations

Band: VHF low (12.5 kHz channel spacing)

Frequency (MHz)	Allocation
71.5125—72.7875	Mobile Tx
76.9625—77.5000	Mobile Tx
85.0125—86.2875	Base Tx
86.9625—87.5000	Base Tx
86.3000—86.7000	Single simplex

COMMENT: Split frequency simplex separation usually either 10 MHz or 13.5 MHz

Band: VHF mid (12.5 kHz channel spacing)

Frequency (MHz)	Allocation
105.00626—107.89375	Base Tx
138.00625—140.99375	Mobile Tx

COMMENT: Split frequency separation usually 33 MHz. This band will be phased out by the end of 1995 to make way for FM broadcasting.

Band: VHF high (12.5 kHz channel spacing)

Frequency (MHz)	Allocation
165.05—168.25	Base Tx
169.85—173.05	Mobile Tx
168.95—169.85	Single simplex

COMMENT: Split frequency separation usually 4.8 MHz

Band: VHF band 1

Frequency (MHz)	Allocation
47.000—68.000	To be announced

COMMENT: Various sub-bands between these two frequencies will be announced shortly. This band is available as the result of the shutdown of 405-line television transmitters.

Table 7.16 *continued*

Band: VHF band 3 (12.5 kHz channel spacing)

Frequency (MHz)	Allocation
184.50–191.50	Mobile Tx
192.50–199.50	Mobile Tx
216.50–223.50	Mobile Tx
176.50–183.50	Base Tx
200.50–207.50	Base Tx
208.50–215.50	Base Tx
174.00–176.50	Single simplex
183.50–184.50	Single simplex
191.50–192.50	Single simplex
199.50–200.50	Single simplex
207.50–208.50	Single simplex
215.50–216.50	Single simplex
223.50–225.00	Single simplex

COMMENT: All these allocations are new and provisional so it is unlikely they will be in full use for some years. Split frequency separation will be 8.0 MHz.

Band: UHF band (12.5 kHz channel spacing)

Frequency (MHz)	Allocation
425.025–425.475	Mobile Tx
425.525–428.975	
445.525–445.975	Base Tx
440.025–443.475	
446.025–446.475	Single simplex

COMMENT: Split frequency separation either 14.5 MHz or 20.5 MHz.

Band: UHF London (12.5 kHz channel spacing)

Frequency (MHz)	Allocation
431.00625–431.99375	Mobile Tx
448.00625–448.99375	Base Tx

COMMENT: This band is only available in the London area. Split frequency separation is 17 MHz

Table 7.17 VHF radiophone band allocated frequencies (12.5 kHz channel spacing — 4.5 MHz separation)

Frequency (MHz)	Allocation
158.53125—159.9125	Mobile Tx
163.0375—164.4250	Base Tx

Table 7.18 UHF cellular band allocated frequencies (25 kHz channel spacing — 45.0 MHz separation)

Frequency (MHz)	Allocation
890.0125—904.9875	Mobile Tx
935.0125—949.9875	Base Tx

Wide area paging

This service provides for one way transmissions from a base station to a small pocket receiver. The transmission is coded to activate only the required pager. The simplest form of pagers merely emit a bleeping sound to alert the holder that they are wanted. Some of the more sophisticated types can receive a short digital message that appears on a small liquid crystal display. Wide area pagers usually cover a specific area such as a town but one service, run by British Telecom, covers most of the country. Wide area paging should not be confused with 'on-site' paging.

Table 7.19 lists wide area paging allocated frequencies.

Table 7.19 Wide area paging allocated frequencies

Band	Frequency (MHz)
VHF (12.5 kHz spacing)	153.025—153.475
UHF (25 kHz spacing)	454.0125—454.825

On-site paging

Similar to wide area paging but low powered and operating over a small area such as a factory, building site, hotel, etc. Sometimes the pager has a small and simple transmitter which allows the user to acknowledge that the paging signal has been received. AM or FM modes may be transmitted, and data communications are possible.

Table 7.20 lists on-site paging allocated frequencies and services. At VHF a 12.5 kHz channel spacing is used, at UHF 25 kHz.

Table 7.20 On-site paging allocated frequencies

Band	Frequency (MHz)	Allocation
VHF	26.957— 27.283	Private paging
	31.725— 31.775	Hospital paging
	161.000—161.100	(acknowledge)
UHF	459.100—459.500	Private paging

Message handling

Many smaller companies may not be able to justify the cost of their own radio-telephone network and so, instead, may make use of a message handling service in which messages are verbally passed between mobile and portable transceivers, through a central contractor. Some message handling services work in a restricted area such as a town or city, but some do span most of the country by using base stations in strategic places.

Table 7.21 lists allocated frequencies for message handling services.

Table 7.21 Message handling services' allocated frequencies

Frequency (MHz)	Allocation
157.4500—158.4000	Mobile Tx
159.9375—160.5375	
162.0500—163.0000	Base Tx
164.4375—165.0375	

Land emergency services

Land emergency services are normally police, fire and ambulance services. Some services are also found on bands allocated to PMR but nearly all police forces operate in bands allocated to the UK Home Office. In addition to the bands listed in Table 7.22, some emergency services in some areas may be located in government mobile allocations (see Tables 7.1 and 7.2). Note that, in accordance with international agreements, the

Table 7.22 Land emergency services' bands and allocated frequencies

Band: VHF low (12.5 kHz channel spacing, AM)

Frequency (MHz)	Allocation
70.50–71.50	Single simplex

Band: VHF mid (12.5 kHz channel spacing, FM)

Frequency (MHz)	Allocation
80.00–84.00	Mobile Tx Single simplex
97.60–102.10	Base Tx

Band: VHF high (12.5 kHz channel spacing, AM/FM)

Frequency (MHz)	Allocation
143.00–144.00	Mobile Tx
152.00–153.00	Base Tx
146.00–149.00	Mobile Tx
154.00–156.00	Base Tx

Band: UHF low (12.5 kHz channel spacing, FM)

Frequency (MHz)	Allocation
420.00–425.00	
429.00–432.00	
443.50–445.00	
446.00–450.00	
459.50–470.00	

Band: UHF high (25 kHz channel spacing, FM)

Frequency (MHz)	Allocation
862.00–864.00	

COMMENT: Usually split frequency simplex but channel pairings vary.

allocation between 97.60 and 102.10 MHz is being re-allocated for broadcast use. Some services have already moved off this band and others will do so over the next few years.

Citizens' band radio

Citizens' band radio communications originated in the USA where it was felt there was a need for a low powered, short distance communication system. The idea was for a low cost service with the minimum of regulations where the user did not have to comply with strict licensing conditions to prove an essential use for two-way radio. Originally it was to give such people as small businesses, servicemen, truckers, farmers and social organisations as a means of communications.

Later, CB acquired a cult following and a colourful slang language all of its own. These days it bears little resemblance to its original aims.

Legal and illegal

The UK started off with an illegal CB service using the same channel allocations as those in the USA. AM equipment, designed for America, was smuggled into Britain. CB became such a craze that thousands of illegal transceivers were in use and often caused havoc to legitimate users of the frequencies which included radio modellers, paging systems and meteorological equipment. Finally, the Government, which appeared reluctant to establish a legal service, gave in. The service introduced in November 1981 had slightly different frequencies to the American equipment and used frequency modulation.

Britain has two CB allocations, one at HF the other at UHF (see Table 7.23). Even so, American equipment, still illegal in the UK, is used from time to time, particularly when conditions favour long distance contact. The UHF allocation tends not to attract many users because of the high cost of the equipment involved. Aerial systems are also more critical and costly at these frequencies.

Range

Across open country useable HF ranges of up to 20 or more miles can be expected but a lot will depend on circumstances, ie, base/base, base/mobile or mobile/mobile working. Ranges are considerably reduced in built-up areas but under lift conditions ranges may become almost global. The band is very prone to the effects of the 11 year sunspot cycle (which will start to lift again around 1987). When that happens it should not be unusual to hear transmissions from the USA, Australia, Asia, South America, etc.

On the UHF band, activity is usually limited to local conditions, but even at these high frequencies lift conditions do occur. For instance, cross channel contacts between stations in southern England and the Channel Islands (distances of more than 100 miles) regularly take place in the summer months.

Note that HF ranges quoted are only likely to be achieved by using a proper CB aerial. Most discone-type aerials, favoured for scanner operation, operate quite poorly at lower frequencies. The same, in fact,

Table 7.23 UK (and USA) CB channels and allocated frequencies

Channel	UK/HF (FM)	Frequencies (MHz) UK/UHF (FM)	CEPT (FM)
01	27.60125	934.01	26.965
02	27.61125	934.06	26.975
03	27.62125	934.11	26.985
04	27.63125	934.16	27.005
05	27.64125	934.21	27.015
06	27.65125	934.26	27.025
07	27.66125	934.31	27.035
08	27.67125	934.36	27.055
09	27.68125	934.41	27.065
10	27.69125	934.46	27.075
11	27.70125	934.51	27.085
12	27.71125	934.56	27.105
13	27.72125	934.61	27.115
14	27.73125	934.66	27.125
15	27.74125	934.71	27.135
16	27.75125	934.76	27.155
17	27.76125	934.81	27.165
18	27.77125	934.86	27.175
19	27.78125	934.91	27.185
20	27.79125	934.96	27.205
21	27.80125		27.215
22	27.81125		27.225
23	27.82125		27.255
24	27.83125		27.235
25	27.84125		27.245
26	27.85125		27.265
27	27.86125		27.275
28	27.87125		27.285
29	27.88125		27.295
30	27.89125		27.305
31	27.90125		27.315
32	27.91125		27.325
33	27.92125		27.335
34	27.93125		27.345
35	27.94125		27.355
36	27.95125		27.365
37	27.96125		27.375
38	27.97125		27.385
39	27.98125		27.395
40	27.99125		27.405

goes for UHF ranges, where an ordinary discone cannot compete with a multi-element Yagi aerial pointed at the transmitting station.

Space satellites

Even old hands at scanning, like myself, still get a kick out of hearing signals from space — even if they are not voice transmissions. For that reason I have included here a wide range of frequency allocations which should enable scanner users to pick up at least some signals.

A large amount of hardware now circles the earth in the form of man-made satellites. Some of these devices stay permanently in space (communication, weather and navigation vehicles); others, such as the American space shuttle, only stay up for a pre-determined period. The latter are usually manned with crews; astronauts in the case of the Americans, cosmonauts in the case of the Russians.

For the scanner user, not all forms of transmission can be received from these space vehicles as many of the frequencies used are in the SHF band (3–30 GHz). However *some* VHF and UHF frequencies are used and those likely to be of interest to scanner users are some of the voice communications for the astronauts/cosmonauts, amateur communications relays and weather satellites. The latter transmit pictures back to earth in digital form which, unfortunately, means the received signal cannot just be fed straight into a television set. However, some home computers can be used with suitable software programs to convert the signals into a picture.

Various other transmissions

Many of the 'space' allocations shown in Tables 7.1 and 7.2 do not contain transmissions of interest. Many satellites transmit streams of data from on-board sensors, used for a variety of scientific measurements, and without suitable decoding equipment these signals are meaningless. The same is true of satellites used for navigation purposes. Also, most of the communications and television satellites, both for relay and broadcasting, operate at frequencies well removed from the coverage of most scanners.

Satellite reception problems

By the time satellite transmissions reach earth they are very weak. In some instances it is necessary to use special aerials to receive the signals. Remembering the comments in Chapter 5 about aerials and polarisation, one problem in the reception of an orbiting satellite's transmissions is that, as the satellite moves, its aerial effectively changes polarity in relation to the aerial of the ground station, causing the received signal to, apparently, fade away and then come back again, every few minutes.

This can be overcome, though, by using a crossed dipole aerial and, again, you should refer to Chapter 5 for more details.

Movement of the space craft also causes an effect, known as doppler shift, which slightly alters the received frequency of the radio signal. This can be a nuisance as it means a scanner must be tuned off the centre frequency to track the shifting signal. On some scanners, such as the Yaesu, AOR-2002 and Icom, this presents no great problem as, fortunately, the manual tuning control can be used to track the signal. On the AOR-2001 and similar scanners it may be possible to completely overcome the effect by switching to wide FM reception mode, although this will not work if other signals are present on adjacent channels.

Amateur satellites

Amateur satellite transmissions are among some of the easiest to receive as the satellites are designed to transmit on frequencies that are easily picked up by unsophisticated equipment. Two satellites that can be received with just a simple aerial are UOSATs 1 & 2, on 145.825 MHz. The satellites were built by amateurs at the University of Surrey and, although they are mostly used for sending down data in ASCII computer code, they also have an interesting on-board voice synthesiser. This can be heard as a robot-type voice listing strings of numbers.

UOSAT transmissions might not be very exciting but they do make a good starting point to get the feel of satellite reception. Aerial phasing and doppler shift problems will all become apparent. Bear in mind that UOSATs are orbiting satellites and so transmissions can only be received for a few minutes at a time unless sophisticated trackable beam aerials are used to follow them from horizon to horizon. Occasionally their orbits take them well away from the UK and, at such times, it might not be possible to receive transmissions at all. In addition to their VHF transmission they also transmit signals on UHF, but in the author's experience these are much more difficult to receive.

Amateur communications satellite transmissions are more interesting but they are also harder to receive. It is necessary to, at least, use a set of crossed dipoles, if not a Yagi aerial, with motors to control direction and elevation.

The way communications take place using these communications satellites is that an amateur transmits up to the satellite on an 'uplink' frequency. The satellite then re-transmits the signal back on a different, 'downlink', frequency. In this way it is quite easy to span large distances using VHF and UHF: communications between Europe and the Americas are quite normal.

This method of re-transmitting the signal is known as 'transponding'. The UOSATs do not have transponders as they are experimental scientific satellites and their job is merely to transmit data from on-board sensors.

Table 7.24 Amateur satellite frequencies

Vehicle	Beacons	Transponder downlink
RS-5	29.330 & 29.452	29.41–29.45
RS–7	29.340 & 29.501	29.46–29.50
RS–10/11	29.357, 29.403, 29.407, 29.453, 145.857, 145.903, 145.907, 145.953	29.36–29.40 145.860–145.900
OSCAR–9	145.825, 435.025	
OSCAR–10	145.810, 145.987	145.830–145.970
OSCAR–11	145.826, 435.025	
FO12	435.797 & 435.913	435.797–435.910

Table 7.24 lists amateur satellites, together with allocated frequencies. With the exception of Oscar 10, all of the satellites are standard orbiting types. Oscar 10 operates in an elliptical orbit which means that it may remain in range for several hours. The RS series are Russian-built while the others have been made by the voluntary organisation, AMSAT.

The frequencies of most interest to scanner users are the downlink ones, but it should be noted that often some, if not all, of the satellites are in orbits that are out of UK range, and satellites are occasionally switched off for long periods, to allow for such things as battery charging from their solar panels.

Some of the RS series satellites are coming to the end of their useful life and Oscar 10 is out of control.

Weather satellites

Most people will be familiar with weather satellite pictures now commonly used during television weather forecasts, These pictures are transmitted from satellites in a coded fashion: circuits in the satellite break the picture up into small segments which are then transmitted as a stream of audio tones. Upon reception at the ground station, these tones must be decoded and segments re-assembled back into a picture. Sophisticated receiving equipment is available for the job, but it is possible to use a home computer to get very acceptable results for a fraction of the price.

At least three companies in the UK, Maplin, Cirkit and Halbar, can supply software for the BBC-B computer for weather picture decoding and assembly. However, it should be noted that although these signals are quite easy to receive, they are fairly wide band and computer pictures will only be possible with a scanner that has an intermediate frequency bandwidth of at least 30 kHz in FM mode. Scanners such as the AORs, Yaesu and Icom are suitable. For anyone with the technical knowledge it is not too difficult to change the IF filters on any scanner to achieve wider bandwidth.

Table 7.25 Weather satellite frequencies

Satellite	Frequency (MHz)	Comments
Meteor 1/30	137.020	Russian
Cosmos 1766	137.400	Russian
Meteor 2/16	137.400	Russian
Meteor 2/14 & 2/15	137.850	Russian
NOAA10	137.500	US sat
NOAA9/11	137.620	11 due in summer 1988

Details of weather satellites are listed in Table 7.25, even though the average scanner user will not have facilities to convert them into pictures. Most scanner users will find the details useful if only to check that they can receive signals direct from space. Several weather satellites can be heard in the 137 MHz band, but it should be noted that they are only switched on at certain times.

Table 7.26 Miscellanous satellite VHF & UHF frequencies

Satellite/vehicle	Frequency (MHz)	Comments
SALYUT 7	142.420	Voice (FM)
	166.000	Robot/Beacon
MIR	143.625	Voice (FM)
	166.140	Robot/Beacon
NASA Shuttles	259.700	Voice (AM)
	296.800	Voice (AM)
Military Comms	235.000–273.000	Various
Navigation Satellites	149.000–150.050	Beacons (CICADA)
	399.000–400.050	Beacons (TRANSIT)

Miscellaneous satellites

A look at the frequency allocations in Tables 7.1 and 7.2 shows that several bands are allocated for space and satellite operation. Many of these bands have little, if any, activity and in recent years as technology has progressed, space communications have tended to move to higher frequencies — usually of several thousand megahertz. Even so, there is occasionally voice traffic in some of the VHF bands and a list of typical users is given in Table 7.26. Do note, though, that they might not always carry transmissions. For instance two frequencies are shown for the NASA space shuttle but on any one flight this band might never be used. Keen space communications fans know that this side of the hobby often means much patience. If at first you hear nothing, try, try and try again.

In the two very narrow navigation satellite bands shown in Table 7.26 it will occasionally be possible to hear either the Russian 'CICADA' system or the USA's 'TRANSIT' service. In the UK reception of 'CICADA' signal transmissions is usually possible several times a day. They are AM signals sounding like fast morse code.

English is the most internationally accepted language in radio communications, yet many communicators appear to have a language all of their own. There is a good reason for some of the codes, abbreviations and expressions that are used on the air: so that misunderstandings can be avoided. The use of a set of common expressions means that even people who speak different languages can make and receive basic messages correctly. In some cases, however (CB being a good example), the expressions used are just part of the folklore which goes with the medium.

We shall first consider some things that are common to most operators.

Phonetic alphabet

Sometimes, under difficult conditions, it maybe impossible to tell what the user transmitting from another station is saying. Under such circumstances it is usual to spell out the message, coding the letters as words, using the 'phonetic alphabet':

A	Alpha	N	November
B	Bravo	O	IOscar
C	Charlie	P	Papa
D	Delta	Q	Quebec
E	Echo	R	Romeo
F	Foxtrot	S	Sierra
G	Golf	T	Tango
H	Hotel	U	Uniform
I	India	V	Victor
J	Juliet	W	Whisky
K	Kilo	X	X-ray
L	Lima	Y	Yankee
M	Mike	Z	Zulu

These phonetics are widely used in callsigns. For instance, amateur station G7XYZ would be Golf Seven X-Ray Yankee Zulu. Similar use of phonetics will be heard in aircraft callsigns which are usually made up of a string of letters with the first or first two letters, denoting the country of registration.

Some expressions are common to most radio users:

Roger An almost universal expression meaning 'I understand or acknowledge receipt of your message'.

Wilco Not quite as common as *Roger*. It means I **will co**mply with your instructions.

Copy A message or part of it. For instance, the expression 'I copy you' means I am able to understand you, I hear you.

Mayday The international call of distress. The word is repeated three times and means that an emergency situation has occurred. All stations on the frequency, except that calling *Mayday* and that providing assistance, must observe strict radio silence.

Pan-Pan A call indicating that assistance is required urgently but no one is in immediate danger.

Affirmative Means yes.

Negative Means no.

Time

Even within the relatively close confines of Europe many countries may be in different time zones and so a standard time system has been adopted so that complex calculations can be avoided during radio communications: Greenwich mean time (GMT). However there is a move afoot to re-name GMT as the universal time constant (UTC). This will be the same time as measured at Greenwich, but the name change will satisfy those who objected to GMT as being a reminder of the days of the British Empire and colonialism.

Occasionally, some radio operators will refer to GMT as 'Zulu', eg, '1500 hours Zulu' is 3 o'clock in the afternoon. British summer time (BST) is known as 'Alpha', that is, GMT + 1 hour. Virtually all radio traffic references to time are made using the 24 hour clock system.

Amateurs

Amateurs form one of only two groups of radio users (the other is CB) who usually 'transmit blind': that is they put out calls for contact with anyone who happens to be on the same frequency or channel. Professional users, on the other hand, except in emergencies, only put out calls for specific stations. But amateurs, too, might well call up particular stations. And, even when transmitting blind, they may well specify that they only want contacts into a certain area. For instance, it is not unusual under lift conditions to hear UK amateurs calling for contacts on the Continent or even from a specific country. While most amateurs will happily chat to anyone who happens to be on the air many will, at times, only want to work long distances. One of the attractions of the hobby is being able, on occasions, to work not only far flung places but also small countries where there may only be a few amateurs. Such 'catches' are a little bit like a stamp collector finding a rare stamp.

Amateurs use expressions known as 'Q-codes' to abbreviate messages. Some typical Q-codes follow. Note that most can be either a statement or a question, eg, QRP can mean 'shall I reduce my power?' or 'reduce your power', depending on the context of use.

International Q − codes

QRA Name of station. Sometimes you may hear the expression 'QRA locator'. This is a grid system used by amateurs to work out the distances between each other.

QRM Interference. This is 'man-made', such as noise from electrical equipment.

QRN Interference. Natural interference, such as static.

QRP Reducing transmitter power. The expression 'QRP station' means a transmitter that is always operated at very low power. Some amateurs specialise in this kind of operation.

QRT Stop sending/transmitting. A station saying 'I am going QRT' usually means he is closing down.

QRZ Who is calling?

QSB Signals fading.

QSK Can I break in on your contact. Often a query from a station wanting to join in a 'net', that is, a group of amateurs passing conversation back and forth.

QSL Acknowledge receipt.

QSO Communicate or communication. For example 'I had a QSO with a French station'.

QSY Change frequency or channel. For example 'Let us QSY to 144.310 MHz'.

QTH Strictly speaking the position of the station in terms of latitude and longitude. Often used, though, to simply refer to wherever the station is by naming the town, village, etc.

There are many other Q-codes but they are rarely used by amateurs using speech for communications.

Reporting codes

Amateurs, like other radio users, have a system of reporting on the signal that they receive. The other station will usually find this information useful as it can tell him what propagation conditions are like and if his equipment is performing correctly. Unlike most scanners, amateur radio transceivers usually have a signal strength meter to indicate received signal strength. The lower part of the scale is usually marked from 0 to 9, above this the scale is marked in decibels (dB). The internationally recognised method of reporting on signals is known as the 'RST code': R is readability, S is signal strength and T is tone. For speech communication the T is not used as it applies only to morse code.

Amateurs will usually be heard to say something like 'you are four by seven'. That means readability 4, signal strength 7.

The code follows:

Readability
R1 Unreadable
R2 Barely readable
R3 Readable with considerable difficulty
R4 Readable with practically no difficulty
R5 Perfectly readable

Signal strength
S1 Faint, barely perceptible
S2 Very weak
S3 Weak
S4 Fair
S5 Fairly good
S6 Good
S7 Moderately strong
S8 Strong
S9 Extremely strong
S9-
+ Meter needle on the end of the scale.

The last one is an unofficial code but often used and a corresponding measurement may be given in decibels, eg, 'You are 20 dB over 9'.

Call sign prefixes

It is possible to identify the country from which a station is transmitting by the first few letters and/or numbers of the callsign. Table 8.1 lists typical countries whose stations may be heard in the UK under some lift conditions.

Contest stations

Occasionally you may hear contests in operation. Participating stations, operated by an individual or a group, are required to make as many

Table 8.1 Amateur callsign prefixes, with associated countries

Prefix	Country	Prefix	Country
C31	Andorra	OE	Austria
CN	Morocco	OH	Finland
CT1,4	Portugal	OHO	Aaland Island
CT2	Azores	OJO	Market Reef
DA,DL	F.R. Germany	OK,OL	Czechoslovakia
DM,Y2—9	D.R. Germany	ON	Belgium
EA	Spain	OY	Faroe Island
EA6	Balearic Isle	OZ	Denmark
EA8	Canary Isle	PA—PI	Netherlands
EA9	Ceuta/Mellila	SK,SM	Sweden
EI,EJ	Eire	SV	Greece
EL	Liberia	SV9	Crete
F	France	TA	Turkey
FC	Corsica	TF	Iceland
G	England	UA	USSR
GD	Isle of Man	UB5,UT5	Ukraine
GI	N. Ireland		
GJ	Jersey (CI)	UP2	Lithuania
GM	Scotland	UQ2	Latvia
GU	Guernsey (CI)	UR2	Estonia
GW	Wales	YO	Rumania
HA,HG	Hungary	YU,YT	Yugoslavia
HB	Switzerland	ZB2	Gibraltar
HBO	Liechenstein	3A	Monaco
HV	Vatican City	3V8	Tunisia
I	Italy	4UI	United Nations
LA,LB	Norway	7X	Algeria
LX	Luxembourg	9A	San Marino
LZ	Bulgaria	9H	Malta

contacts as possible within a given space of time. The biggest such contest in the UK is the VHF National Field Day (NFD) organised by the Radio Society of Great Britain, which takes place every year on the first week-end in July between 3.00 pm on the Saturday and 3.00 pm on the Sunday. During the event the whole spectrum around 144.300 MHz comes alive with thousands of transmitting stations. Unfortunately, most of the transmissions are SSB so will only be of interest to owners of more expensive scanners. However, for such owners this event usually provides an occasion to hear a lot of long distance stations. Lift conditions are normally good at this time of year and many continental stations beam their transmission towards the UK to take part in the contest.

Special event stations

Occasionally you may hear 'special event stations' which are usually operated by a group of amateurs such as an amateur radio club. They are granted a special one-off callsign to celebrate special events such as a country fair. Callsigns are often granted to have some significance to the event. For instance, amateurs operating from the Totnes Agricultural Fair might use the callsign GB2TAF. The GB prefix is the normal one used for special event stations although during the Victory-in-Europe celebrations during 1985, the GV prefix was used in the callsigns of associated stations.

Repeaters

Details of how repeaters work were outlined in Chapter 2. Repeaters in the 2 metre and 70 centimetre bands operate in FM mode and so can be received on any scanner that covers the bands. They are recognised as a regular transmission of morse code containing the two letters which identify which repeater they are. Amateurs often call blind on repeaters and you may well hear the expression 'This is GUIDKD listening through WD'. That means that amateur station GUIDKD has accessed the repeater with callsign WD and is awaiting any replies.

Marine

The international VHF marine band as we saw in Chapter 7 is channellised. The standard procedure at commencement of any transmission on the band is to first put out a call on channel 16: the calling and distress channel, requesting contact with a particular station. When that station replies, both then move to a 'working channel'.

This method of operation means that at any time there are hundreds of stations listening to channel 16, and so if any boat or ship needs help someone is bound to hear the call. A further advantage is that it enables shore stations to make general broadcasts to ships informing them of weather information, safety warnings and lists of ships (traffic lists) for whom there are telephone link calls. These transmissions are not made on channel 16 but the shore station tells ships which channel or channels to move to.

Vessels licensed for marine RT are given a callsign comprising letters, numbers or both, depending on where the ship is registered. Generally the official callsign is only used , however, when establishing link calls. For other contacts the vessel will only usually give the ship or boat's name.

Photograph 8(a) A busy modern port needs radio communication to co-ordinate the movement and berthing of hundreds of trawlers, pleasure craft, ferries and cargo ships.

Securité

Pronounced 'securitay' this word, repeated three times, precedes any broadcast transmission where there is reference to safety. Again, broadcasts telling ships that there is a securite message will be broadcast on channel 16, will give the channel to move to for the details.

Securité broadcasts usually concern 'navigational warnings'. Typically they might inform vessels that a certain beacon or lighthouse is out of action, or they might warn of floating obstructions such as cargo washed off a ship's deck or a capsized vessel.

Some shore stations have the task of making regular broadcasts in busy shipping areas where there may be a need to pass frequent safety messages. Typical is Cherbourg Radio (channel 11) which transmits safety information every half hour for the southern part of the English Channel — possibly the busiest shipping zone in the world.

Weather

All coastal stations transmit regular weather forecasts and gale warnings. Again, forewarning of a weather forecast or gale warning will be made on channel 16 and the station will say which working channels will carry the forecast.

More localised forecasts are made by some ports, using the same procedure as the coastal station. Normally such forecasts are broadcast on the regular port operations channel.

Port operations

So far we have looked largely at the kind of transmissions and broadcasts that are from coastal stations covering a wide area. However, the marine VHF band is also used for other kinds of contact, in particular port operations. Many ports are busy places and some have traffic handling facilities almost as sophisticated as airports.

Typical radio traffic concerns departure and arrival of ships, ferries and pleasure craft. Port controllers, for example, may have to hold some ships off-shore until other ships have left and made space for them. They may be contacted by yachts wanting mooring spaces in marinas. Other tasks involve liaison with bodies such as customs and immigration officers.

Ship-to-ship

Several channels are set aside for ship-to-ship use. These are used for a variety of purposes: anything from the local yacht club marshalling a dinghy race to trawlermen discussing where the best catches are.

Emergencies

Britain has probably the best marine emergency services in the world; its tradition as a seafaring nation is probably responsible for this. The waters around the British Isles are covered by lifeboat and coastguard stations, and back-up to these services comes from the Air Force and Royal Navy. All services are on call to assist with emergencies at sea.

The first warning of an emergency will come with a Mayday call. This is internationally recognised and will be made on channel 16. Normally, a coastal station or port will receive the call and put the emergency services into action. Where coastal stations are out of range, a ship may well respond to the Mayday. During this time all traffic, other than emergency traffic, is supposed to cease on channel 16. It is sad, however, that some radio operators ignore this and it is not unusual for the emergency services to have their messages jammed by ship's operators who appear to consider their own relatively trivial messages more important than other people's lives.

No two emergencies are the same. In some instances it may just be a small vessel lost in fog and worried about running onto rocks. In such cases coastal stations might be able to offer position fixes by taking bearings on the transmissions of the vessel in distress pinpointing the vessel's position.

At the other end of the scale, the emergency might be a ship sinking in a storm. The crew may have abandoned the vessel and be in the water or on liferafts. On these occasions all emergency services may be involved. An RNLI lifeboat may be on the scene, helicopters from the nearest naval station sweeping the sea for survivors and overhead an RAF coastal command Nimrod with its massively powerful search-lights lighting up the area. It's also quite likely that other ships in the area may come to the scene to assist.

All this requires communications if the efforts of all services are to be co-ordinated. While the coastal station will act as the main co-ordination centre, at the scene of the rescue the various groups involved will need to communicate, too. In UK waters, the lifeboat remains in contact with the coastal station on channel 0 — the helicopters and aircraft will probably be on this channel as well. Normal commercial vessels are *not* permitted to use this channel so they will stay on channel 16. The coastal station and lifeboat may therefore have to work both channels. Some lifeboats and coastguard vessels are fitted with aircraft band equipment to provide communications on the airband search and rescue and emergency frequencies (see Chapter 7).

Communications on the marine bands are, by and large, carried out in plain language. The few expressions and procedures described are the only likely exceptions.

Aviation

The world of aviation is the winner when we come to judge it in terms of the number of expressions and jargon. However, little of it is trivial. Aircraft crew cope with a variety of complex situations and may well be flying in and out of countries where air traffic controllers have little if any understanding of the English language.

Like the marine band the aircraft band is channelised, but the channels are referred to by their actual frequency and not by a channel number. The procedure for contacting a station is also very different. There is no common calling channel: a pilot wanting to call a ground station simply looks up the frequency and calls on it.

Callsigns

All civilian aircraft have a registration. In some instances this will consist solely of letters with the first letter or letters denoting the country of registration. In other instances, such as aircraft registered in the USA the registration may be a letter followed by numbers. Generally, privately owned light aircraft or those operated as air-taxis will use their registration as their radio callsign.

Normal procedure for making contact with the ground station will be to give the full callsign. The controller will reply, perhaps, referring to the aircraft by the full callsign, in which case the pilot will again, when transmitting, use the full callsign. At some stage though, for the sake of brevity, the approach controller will just use the last two letters and from then on the pilot will do the same.

Photograph 8(b) Typical radio station on a light aircraft. The radio console is the stack in the centre. From top to bottom: DME (distance measuring equipment), console selector (allows pilot to chose which radio output goes to his headset), Navcom one (communication frequency on the left window, for navigation on the right), NAVCOM 2, and transponder.

Larger aircraft, such as those used on regular passenger carrying routes, may use the same type of callsign, or a special callsign based on the airline's name and typically may also use the flight number for that service. Again the ground controller will probably, at some stage, abbreviate this and just use the number: from then on the aircrew will do the same.

Numbers preceded by the word 'Ascot' denote the callsign of a British military aircraft flying on a civilian route. The USAF equivalent is the pre-fix 'Mac'.

Landing instructions

First contact an aircraft has with an airfield is usually on the approach frequency. After transmitting on the frequency and identifying the aircraft, the pilot usually gives aircraft position and altitude. The approach controller then transmits information relating to airfield barometric presure (QFE), the wind direction and speed, the runway in use (runways are always identified by the compass heading needed to land on them), and details of other aircraft in the landing pattern or about to take off. Temperature and visibility in kilometres may be also given. If the weather is bad the RVR (runway visual range) may be referred to. The pilot needs to know the QFE (sometimes just called the 'fox echo') so that the aircraft's altimeter may be set so that it will read zero feet at runway level. Other information such as runway state (if affected by rain, ice or snow) may be transmitted, followed by instructions to remain at present altitude or start descending to circuit height (often about 1000 feet). Some of this information the pilot will repeat back.

As the aircraft gets closer to the airport there will come a stage where the approach controller instructs the pilot to change to the tower frequency. The pilot always repeats the frequency to be changed to: this is standard procedure when changing frequency at any point in a flight.

Now the pilot calls the tower and again will give his position and altitude. The aircraft may be making a straight-in approach, that is, arriving at the airfield in line with the runway or he may be 'joining the circuit'. The circuit is an imaginary path around the airfield in the form of a racetrack. It can be in a lefthand or righthand direction and, once joined, the pilot will report at various stages such as downwind leg, base leg and finals. Finals occur at a given distance from the runway and the pilot will always tell the controller when the aircraft is one mile out. Throughout this stage of the flight the pilot will be given various instructions and updated QFE, wind speed and direction information. At any stage of the approach the pilot may be told to divert course because the controller cannot yet fit him in with other traffic. The instruction may be to briefly orbit over a given position, or to fly out further to a given point and then re-join the landing pattern.

Once on the ground the pilot may be told to change frequency yet again (particularly at larger airfields), this time to speak to the ground handler. Here, instructions on which taxiways to use and where to park the aircraft will be given.

SRA and PAR radar let-down

Occasionally, in bad visibility, a pilot may need to be 'talked-down'. SRA (surveillance radar approach) may be used to give the pilot precise instructions to reach the end of the runway. Normally, the airfield has a special frequency for this and once the pilot has established contact with the controller there is a point when the controller tells the pilot not to acknowledge further instructions. From then on, the controller gives the pilot a running commentary on the aircraft's position in relation to an imaginary line drawn outwards from the runway, known as the 'centre-line'. Compass headings may be given to the pilot, to steer the aircraft, in order to get on to the centre-line. Other information given tells the pilot how far the aircraft is from the runway and what height it should be at. At a point about half a mile from the runway, the controller announces that the approach is complete. If the pilot cannot see the runway at this stage the approach must be abandoned for another, or the aircraft is diverted to another airfield. Failing to touch-down results in a 'go-around' (formerly an 'overshoot').

PAR (precision radar approach) is similar, but also tells the pilot altitude and whether or not the aircraft is on the 'glide slope'.

Startup

The procedure at the start of a flight varies from airfield to airfield. On smaller airfields the pilot may start the aircraft and then ask for take-off instructions. The ground controller transmits details of which runway is in use, QFE and wind, then instructs the pilot to start taxiing to a holding point just before the end of the runway. Once the runway is clear, the controller allows the aircraft to take off and relays other instructions such as which height to climb to and when the aircraft can start turning on course.

At bigger airfields, particularly those in busy flight areas, the procedure may be far more complicated and will depend to some extent on whether the flight is VFR (visual flight rules) or IFR (instrument flight rules). The first, VFR, is where an aircraft flies solely by dead reckoning. In other words, the pilot navigates by using a compass and a map, looking out of the aircraft window for landmarks. The second, IFR, is where the pilot uses radionavigation and instruments to cover the route. Most commercial flights are IFR and such flights are always along designated airways routes. Prior to a flight the pilot files a flight plan with Air Traffic Control which is telexed to controllers on the aircraft's route, who are then aware of the type of aircraft, altitude requested and destination.

At commencement of the flight the pilot informs the tower that all is ready. At this stage the controller may well only say the aircraft is clear to start up and, perhaps, will give the temperature. Once the pilot informs the controller the aircraft is ready for take-off, taxiing instructions, the QFE, the runway in use and the wind details are all given. At this stage or shortly after clearance is given to the pilot, detailing destination, the airways to use and altitudes. In the UK airways are identified by colours (red, blue, green, white, amber) with a number. After the actual take-off, the aircraft may be handed over to another controller, such as approach, before the pilot is finally told to contact 'airways' or 'information' services.

Airways

Busy air routes, such as those over Europe, are divided up into countries and regions which have central control points for all the air routes in the sectors. Although VFR flights at low altitudes can, by and large, choose the course they fly, this is not the case at higher altitudes in the airways. Now we are in the realm of 'controlled airspace' and pilots *must* fly along a certain course at a certain height. The airways are marked at regular points, and where they cross, by beacons on the ground. These are used for navigation purposes and also form what are known as 'compulsory

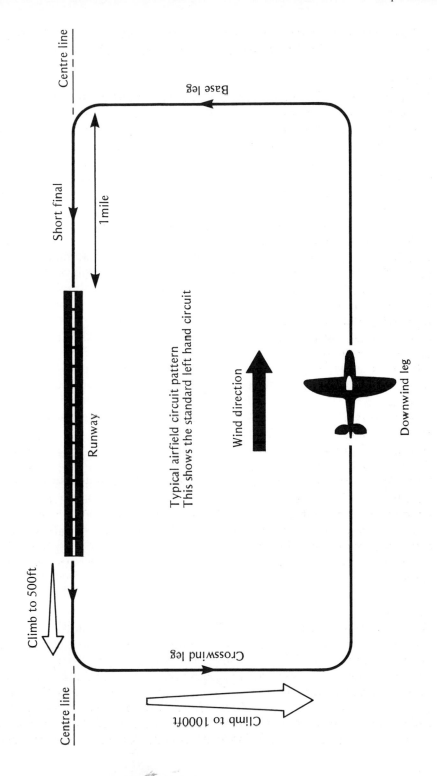

Centre line

Base leg

Short final

1mile

Runway

Typical airfield circuit pattern
This shows the standard left hand circuit

Wind direction

Downwind leg

Climb to 500ft

Crosswind leg

Centre line

Climb to 1000ft

reporting points': as the aircraft passes over a beacon the pilot must report to the sector controller, giving the name of the beacon, flight level (at higher altitudes the height is abbreviated, eg, 10,000 feet becomes 'flight level one-zero-zero'), and 'forward estimate' time for the next reporting point. These points are referred to by the name of the place where the beacon is sited.

Towards the end of the journey the pilot may be given a fairly complex set of instructions. Landing at major airports like London Heathrow may, at busy times, involve joining the 'stack': an imaginary spiral staircase in the sky. The aircraft joins at the top and flies a racetrack shaped circuit, slowly dropping to different flight levels until, at the bottom, it is routed to the airfield

Flight information

Everything above 25,000 feet is 'controlled airspace' (in some regions airspace below that altitude is controlled, too). PIlots can obtain details of traffic movements in the region from the UIR (upper-flight information region) service. Below that level, information is provided by the FIR (flight information region) service. Note that both the UIR and FIR are *advisory* services: they provide information for pilots but do not control the movement of aircraft.

A further advisory service is available for small aircraft on VFR flights: LARS (lower airspace radar service). The facility is provided by the various MATZ (military aerodrome traffic zones) up and down the country. Again, they do not control flights but merely offer information regarding other aircraft in the area.

Company frequencies

Most airlines use 'company frequencies'. Any one frequency, however, may be used by several airline operators to contact company ground stations. An example of the use of company frequencies could be when an aircraft wishes to contact the operations department of the company base at the destination airfield, in order to give the estimated time of arrival or request special services such as wheelchairs for invalid passengers. Other messages may concern servicing required on the aircraft: instruments may need adjusting, or there may be minor technical problems that engineers will need to correct before the aircraft takes-off again.

Glossary

The following list of abbreviations and expressions are regularly used during typical transmissions between ground and air.

Abort Abandon (ie, abandon take-off).
AFIS Airfield flight information service.

AIREP Report for position and weather in flight.
Airway Defined flight path.
amsl Above mean sea level.
APU Auxiliary power unit (backup when engines are off).
ASDA Runway accelerated stop distance.
ASI Air speed indicator.
ATA Actual time of arrival.
ATC Air traffic control.
ATIS Automatic terminal information service.
avgas Aviation grade petrol.
Avionics Aircraft electronics.
Backtrack Taxi back down the runway.
Beacon Station transmitting continuous navigation signal.
CAT Clear air turbulence.
CBs Cumulo nimbus (thunder clouds).
Conflicting Conflicting traffic, etc, possible collision course.
Decimal Decimal point as in frequency, eg, 128.65 MHz.
Cav-OK Ceiling and visibility are good.
DF Direction finding by radio.
DME Distance measuring equipment.
Drift Lateral movement off desired track.
ETA Estimated time of arrival.
FIR Flight information region.
Flameout Total power loss on jet or turbo prop engine.
Gear Undercarriage.
Glidepath Line of descent on landing.
GMC Ground movement controller.
GMT Greenwich mean time.
Go around Overshoot runway and re-join circuit.
GPU Ground power unit.
Greens Landing gear down and locked indicators.
Homer Homing beacon.
IAS Indicated air speed.
IFR Instrument flight rules.
ILS Instrument landing system.
IMC Instrument meteorological conditions.
JET A1 Jet and turbo-prop fuel (kerosene).
Knots Nautical miles per hour.
LARS Lower airspace radar service.
Localiser Glidepath beacon.
Mach Speed in relation to the speed of sound.
MATZ Military aerodrome traffic zone.
METAR Meterological report (not a forecast).
Navaid Navigational aid.
NavCom Combined communication and navigation radio.

Navex Navigation exercise (training flight).
NDB Non-directional beacon.
NOTAM Notice to airmen.
Okta An eighth. Used to denote cloud density.
Ops Operations.
Orbit Fly in a circle.
Overshoot No longer used, see 'go around'.
Pax Passengers (eg, 64 pax on board).
PAR Precision approach radar.
PPO Prior permission only (restricted airfields).
QDM Magnetic heading.
QFE Barometric pressure at aerodrome.
QNH Barometric pressure at sea level.
Roll-out Stopping distance after touchdown.
RSR Route surveillance radar.
RVR Runway visual range.
SAR Search and rescue.
SELCAL Selective calling system (activates radio by code).
SID Standard instrument departure.
SIG Significant.
SitRep Situation report.
Squawk Switch transponder on.
Squawk ident Select 'identification' mode on transponder.
SRE Surveillance radar element.
STOL Short take-off and landing.
Stratus Low misty cloud (often obscures runway approach).
TAI True air speed indicator.
TACAN Tactical air navigator.
TAF Terminal area forecast.
TAR Terminal area radar.
TAS True air speed.
TMA Terminal control area.
Traffic Aircraft in flight.
UIR Upper flight information region.
US Unserviceable.
UTC Universal time constant (GMT).
VASI Runway lights angled to give a visual glide slope.
VFR Visual flight rules.
VMC Visual meteorological conditions.
VOLMET Continuous weather forecast.
VOR VHF omni-direction range beacon.
VSI Vertical speed indicator (rate of climb).
VTOL Vertical take-off and landing.
WX Weather.

Scanner and accessories 9
review

A look at some of the equipment currently available in the UK

This chapter is split into two sections; Scanners and Accessories and in the accessories section will be found product details of some specialised aerials.

First the scanners. Included in the list are some scanners which are out of production. In the case of some models such as the AOR-2001 these scanners may still be available through dealers who have existing stocks. In the case of some other scanners such as the Bearcat 220FB, production may have ceased some years ago. However, it was felt worthwhile including some of these models as many of them are widely available on the second-hand market. Where this is the case a rough guide to second-hand prices have been included. These should be fairly accurate at the time of writing (early 1986).

The review gives the features and specifications claimed by the manufacturer. The comments that have been added are my own. However, although I own several scanners the review should not be interpreted as a recommendation for any particular model. It is up to the prospective purchaser to satisfy himself that any claims made by the manufacturer are accurate.

Buying guide

If you have read the book so far you should know by now which features you want on a scanner and should be able to choose the right model from the information given in this chapter.

It is always a good idea to buy a scanner from a dealer who has proper servicing facilities. He may not offer the same discounts as some other cut-price retailers but if you have problems he will be able to sort them out. Dealers who specialise in amateur equipment will as a general rule have the right kind of workshop equipment to carry out scanner repairs.

On the other hand, the corner shop that sells a few TV's, radios and household appliances is not likely to have the kind of test gear needed to check-out and re-align sophisticated VHF/UHF equipment. Never mind what the salesman says, it is a specialised area of servicing.

The right kind of dealer will carry out repairs quickly. The wrong kind will usually send your scanner back to the importers for repair and sometimes this can take weeks or even months. Many retailers will not repair equipment unless it was purchased from them.

Having said all that I am pleased to say that current scanners generally appear to be fairly reliable. Of the six I have owned two developed faults but these were old models and the repairs were not expensive. The others have never let me down even though they've been treated quite roughly at times.

Prices

I have avoided listing prices in this second edition of 'Scanners' as currency fluctuations on world currency markets can lead to quite dramatic price swings. A glance at a current issue of a magazine aimed at the amateur radio or electronic hobbyist market will usually reveal dealer advertisements carrying up to date prices. The small ads' in the same magazines will usually give a good guide to second-hand prices as well.

Model: AOR 2001.
Importer/Agent: Lowe.
Type: Synthesised — base station.
Receiver: Triple conversion/Up conversion.
Coverage: 25—550 MHz (no gaps).
Quoted sensitivity: NFM 0.3 uV (12 dB SINAD).
  WFM 1.0 uV (12 dB SINAD).
  AM 0.5 uV (10 dB S/N).
Selectivity: NEM ±7.5 KHz @6 dB ±20 KHz @ 70 dB
  WFM ±50 KHz @6 dB ±250 KHz @ 60 dB
  AM ±5.0 KHz @6 dB ±10 KHz @ 70 dB
Programming: Key Pad
Modes: NFM, WFM, NAM. Individually programmed on each memory channel.
Number of channels: 20.
Display: LCD with switchable lamp.
Search: Yes. User defined limits. 5.0/12.5/25 KHz step rates.
Priority: Yes, Channel 1.
Delay: Yes. All channels or none.
Lock out: Yes. Individually programmed into memory.
Power source: External 12 Volt or mains adaptor (supplied).
Audio out: 1 Watt.

External connections: Antenna (BNC) — 12 v Power — External speaker.
Manual tuning knob: No.
Dimensions: 138 mm wide, 80 mm high, 200 mm long.
Additional features:

Comments: This has a very wide frequency coverage for such a compact set. The set has two disadvantages: the first is the all-plastic case which makes the set prone to interference from computers, power supply transformers, etc, and the second is the rather slow scanning speed. AOR claim a rate of 20 channels in 4 seconds (still quite slow) but I have timed my own set and two others and they are all worked out at a 6 seconds for 20 channels. Despite those shortcomings, this is a very good receiver.

No longer in production as of late 1985 but existing dealer stocks will probably last well into 1986. The mobile mount and computer interface are optional extras.

Model: AOR-2002
Importer/Agent: Lowe
Type: Synthesised base station.
Receiver: Triple conversion/Up conversion.
Coverage: 25—550 MHz and 800—1300 MHz.
Specifications: See AOR 2001.

Display: LCD (as per AOR 2001) plus bargraph S-Meter.
External Connections: As AOR 2001 but also 16 way IDC connector to take optional RS232 adaptor for external computer control.
Manual tuning knob: Yes. Rotary, click-stop type.
Dimensions: As AOR 2001.

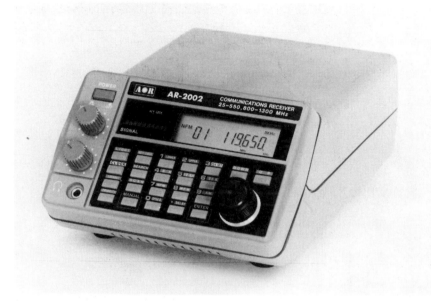

Comments: To all intents and purposes this is the re-vamped version of the AOR 2001. Physically it is identical except for a re-arrangement of the front panel which now includes an LED Bargraph signal meter and a rotary tuning knob. On the back panel is a 16 way IDC chassis plug which mates with the socket on the optional RS232 converter. The back panel also has a small LED lamp to show that external control has been selected.

Bearcats

After a period of some uncertainty and financial problems for the original manufacturers, the Bearcat Scanners are back in production. They are now marketed under the 'Bearcat Uniden' brand name and two models are currently available in the U.K. The first is a base/mobile type receiver, the UBC 175XL and the other is a hand portable, the UBC 100XL.

Many earlier models, such as the classic 220FB, are often seen on the second-hand market and the 220 in particular can still give account of itself. Sensitivity is a bit down on more modern sets like the AOR's and a first IF of 10.7 MHz can lead to image problems. There were one or two common problems such as power supply failure and the lack of FM modes on some bands but in Scanners 2 details are given of how these can be overcome.

Model: Bearcat Uniden UBC 175XL.
Type: Synthesised base/mobile.
Receiver: Double conversion superhetrodyne (IF frequencies not stated).
Coverage: 66–88 MHz FM, 118–136 MHz Air Band AM, 136–174 MHz FM & 406–512 MHz FM.
Sensitivity: 0.4 uV FM (12 dB SINAD)
          0.8 uV AM (12 dB SINAD)
Selectivity: −55 dB @ ± 25 KHz.
Programming: Key Pad.
Modes: AM or FM automatically switched according to frequency.
Number of Channels: 16.
Scan rate: 15 channels per second.
Display: Liquid Crystal Display (LCD).
Search: User defined limits with step rates of either 5 or 12.5 KHz.
Search rate: 25 steps per second.
Priority: Yes.
Delay: Yes. 3 second fixed.
Lock out: Yes.
Power source: 13.8 V DC (500 mA). AC adaptor supplied.
Audio out: 1 Watt @ 8 Ohms.
External connections: 13.8 V DC, external loudspeaker & Antenna (BNC). The obligatory telescopic whip aerial is supplied.
Dimensions: 240 W × 62 H × 180 D (mm). Weighs 740 g.
Comments: Clearly designed for the American market and so the availability of AM solely on Air Band will have drawbacks for some UK users. Otherwise a reasonably priced middle of the range scanner although it's small size and wood grain case do make it look a bit like an executive desk digital clock.

Model: Bearcat Uniden UBC 100XL.
Type: Synthesised Hand-held portable.
Specifications: Coverage, sensitivity and features are all identical to the UBC 175XL except for the following details.
Power source: 7.2 V DC (200 mA). AC adaptor and Ni-Cads provided.
Audio out: 300 mW into 8 Ohms.
Dimensions: 75 W × 35 D × 178 H (mm).
Comments: Supplied with Helical antenna and Ni-Cads (essential). I have no personal experience of this set but have heard favourable comments from owners, particularly those who have used other makes of hand-held and made comparisons.

Model: DR600.
Importer/Agent: Aero Hobby Supplies.
Type: Portable.
Receiver: Single conversion (10.7 MHz).
Coverage: 108–136 MHz.
Quoted sensitivity: 0.5 uV (10 dB S+N/N).
Selectivity: 25 KHz BW @ 6 dB and 140 KHz @ 40 dB.
Programmings: Crystal.
Modes: AM only.
Number of channels: 5.
Display: 5 digit LCD.
Search: Yes. Manual.
Priority: No.
Delay: Not stated.
Lock out: No.
Power source: Internal AA NiCads (supplied), external 12–20 V DC or
AC.
Audio out: 800 mW.
External connections: Antenna (Motorola), external power source/charge
and external speaker/earpiece.
Manual tuning knob. Yes.
Dimensions: 108×76×140 mm.

Additional features: Built-in swivel telescopic aerial. Supplied with NiCads and charger, carry strap, 5 crystals of customers choice and earpiece.

Comments: One of the few British made scanners. The DR600 is an airband-only unit which offers full tuning or scanning of crystal controlled channels. Sturdy all-metal casing and professional performance are reflected in the price which admittedly includes 5 crystals and NiCads. The batteries can be charged whilst the set is being used and a built-in regulator prevents overcharging. Very good three stage AGC.

Model: CR600.
Importer/Agent: Aero Hobby Supplies.
Comments: Again British built and with identical specifications to the DR600 but without the manual tuning facility. It offers 6 crystal controlled channels.

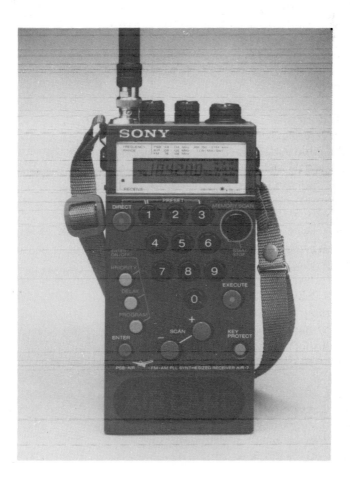

Model: Sony Air-7.

Type: Hand-held portable.

Receiver: Synthesised double Superhetrodyne.

Coverage: 150–2194 kHz AM, 76–108 mHz WBFM, 108–136 mHz AM & 144–174 mHz NBFM.

Programming: Keypad.

Modes: AM, WBFM, NBFM automatically selected according to band.

Number of Channels: 10 per band.

Display: Liquid Crystal Display (LCD).

Search: Bandsearch only.

Delay: Yes.

Priority: Yes.

Power source: 6 V DC from 4 × AA cells. Rechargeable packs, AC and 12 V vehicle adaptors available as an optional extra.

Audio out: 400 mW at 8 Ohms.

External connections: 6 V DC, earphone, Antenna (BNC).

Dimensions: 90 W × 179 H × 50 D (mm). Weighs 600 g.

Comments: Bulky, heavy, limited coverage and expensive. However, Air band fans say it performs superbly and I'm told the AGC (very important with AM) is excellent.

Model: ICOM 1C-R7000.

Importer/Agent: Thanet.

Type: Base/mobile.

Receiver: Quadruple/triple/double conversion.

Coverage: 25–1000 MHz & 1025–2000 MHz no gaps. Specifications are only guaranteed for the 25–1000 MHz range.

Quoted sensitivity: FMN less 0.5 uV (12 dB SINAD)

FMW 20 dB NQL −0 dBu.

AM 10 dB S/N −0 dBu (1 uV) or less.

SSB 10 dB S/N −10 dBu (0.3 uV) or less.

Selectivity: FMN 15 KHz @ 6 dB or 9 KHz @ 6 dB.

AM 9 KHz @ 6 dB.

FMW 150 KHz @ 6 dB.

SSB 2.8 KHz @ 6 dB.

Programming: Key pad.

Modes: FM narrow and wide, narrow AM and SSB.

Number of Channels: 99.

Display: Dual colour fluorescent. Frequency, Mode, etc.

Search: Yes and with autowrite (automatic entry of frequency into memory). 100 Hz+1/5/10/12.5/25 KHz.

Priority: Yes. Programmable.

Delay: No.

Lock out: Yes (selectable scan channels).

Power source: 12 V DC or 240 V AC.

Audio out: 2.5 Watts.
External connections: Full details not specified.
Manual tuning knob: Yes with lock on/off.
Dimensions: 303×127×319 (with projections).
Additional features: Noise blanker, S-Meter, various types of scan (full, programmed, by mode, priority, auto-write, etc). Optional extras include infra-red remote controller, voice synthesised frequency readout, mobile mounting bracket and computer interface.

Comments: It has a massive range of features and very wide coverage. The price is high but this includes most of the circuitry required for external computer control. Thanet say only a simple interface is required and is supplied free in a cable/plug assembly designed to work with the BBC–B computer.

Model: JIL SX-200.
Importer/Agent: Garex.
Type: Synthesised base/mobile.
Receiver: Double conversion (10.7 MHz/455 KHz).
Coverage: 26–88, 108–180, 380–514 MHz.
Quoted sensitivity: FM VHF 0.4 uV (12 dB S/N).
                FM UHF 1.0 uV (12 dB S/N).
                AM VHF 1.0 uV (12 dB S/N).
                AM UHF 2.0 uV (12 dB S/N).

Selectivity: ±25 KHz @ 60 dB.

Programming: Key pad.

Modes: Narrow Am or FM (not programmable onto individual channels).

Number of channels: 16.

Display: Fluorescent.

Search: Yes. User defined limits. Step rate automatically selected; 5 KHz below 58 MHz and 12.5 KHz above 58 MHz.

Priority: No.

Delay: Yes. Not programmable (all or nothing).

Lock out: Yes. Using Scan A or Scan B. Lock out channels are located in Scan B.

Power source: 12 V or mains adaptor (supplied). 2 penlight cells for memory backup.

Audio out: 2 Watts.

External connections: 12 V power. Recorder audio, external speaker, Tape recorder switch (needs external circuit). Antenna (Motorola).

Manual tuning knob: Yes. Fine tune only.

Dimensions:

Additional features: Voice-squelch. Display dimmer.

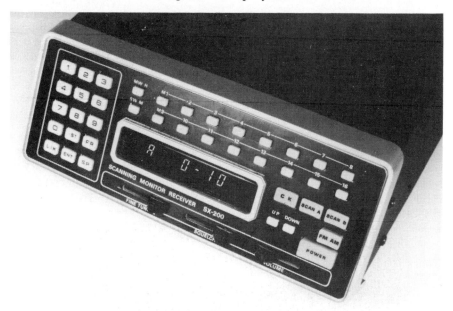

Comments: When it first appeared it offered far more than its competitors but is now starting to show its age. The major drawback with the set is the inability to mix AM and FM. A very robust set, it has a solid metal case which acts as an effective screen against interference. Now rather expensive compared with other sets which offer far greater frequency range, facilities and sensitivity. Widely available on the second-hand market. In the next book, SCANNERS 2, I will be including some add-ons and modifications for this set including a front panel bargraph S-Meter and simultaneous AM/FM circuit.

Model: JIL SX-400.
Importer/Agents: Garex.
Type: Base/Mobile.
Receiver: Double conversion superhet.
Coverage: 26—520 MHz (no gaps).
Quoted sensitivity: VHF FM (S/N=312 dB) 0.5 uV
                         AM (S/N−10 dB) 1.0 uV
               UHF FM (S/N=12 dB) 0.5 uV.
                        AM (S/N=10 dB) 2.0 uV.
Signal/noise ratio: 45 dB.
Selectivity: FM=60 dB at ±15 KHz.
           AM=60 dB at ±10 KHz.
           VHF image rejection=50 dB.
Programming: Keypad.
Modes: AM/FM.
Number of channels: 20.
*Display:*Fluorescent.
Search: Yes. User defined limits.
Priority: Yes (pre-set channel).

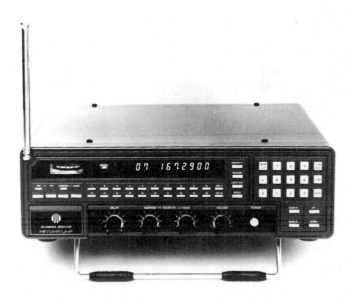

Delay: Yes. 0—4 seconds variable.

Lock out: Yes and scanning can be across some or all 20 channels by allocating channels to either the 'B' block or 'A' (all channels) block.

Power source: 12 V DC or 240 V AC via optional adaptor.

Audio out: 4 Watt.

External connections: Antenna, 10.7 MHz I.F., External speaker, record audio, computer interface (IEEE, RS423 or RS232), external switching (tape recorder, etc), power in, converter/aerial switch socket for optional units.

Manual tuning knob: No.

Dimensions: 300×90×210mm.

Additional features: Signal strength meter, computer control, squelch 'width' selector, AM noise blanker, aerial attenuator and coverage possible from LF to 1.4 GHz with optional converters.

Comments: This is a superbly built scanner but is, I feel, only likely to appeal to professional or commercial users.

Early versions of the SX-400 had very rough sounding audio. It is understood that this was probably due to original batches being fitted with a capacitor of the wrong value and the main retail agents, Revco, say current models do not have this problem and earlier ones can easily have the fault rectified.

Surprisingly the AC adaptor is an extra.

Model: Lowe FS 10.

Importer/Agent: Lowe.

Type: Pocket portable.

Receiver: Double conversion (10.7 MHz/455 KHz).

Coverage: 70—80 MHz or 130—170 MHz (range must be stated when purchasing).

Quoted sensitivity: 0.3 uV (12 dB SINAD).

Selectivity: 12 KHz BW @ 6 dB.

Programming: Crystal.

Modes: FM only.

Number of channels: 10.

Display: LED lamp.

Search: No.

Priority: No.

Delay: No.

Lock out: No.

Power source: 5 V DC from internal NiCad (supplied).

Audio out: 100 mW approx.

External connections: External speaker, antenna (miniature jack) and re-charge.

Manual tuning knob: No.

Dimensions: 127×71×35mm.

Additional features: Manual channel stepping allows selection of any one channel. Leatherette case available as optional extra.
(Also sold under 'NIRECOM' label.)
Comments: Very compact pocket portable. Limited bandwidth coverage limits 70–80 MHz bandwidth and 130–170 MHz version to 4 MHz bandwidth. This means for instance that both the 2 M amateur band and Marine Band could not be covered on the same set. The set is physically identical to the Lowe AP-12.

Model: LOWE AP-12. (Physically identical to Lowe FS-10)
Importer/Agent: Lowe.
Type: Pocket portable.
Receiver: Double conversion (10.7 MHz/455 KHz).
Coverage: 108–136 MHz.
Quoted Sensitivity: 0.5 uV (10 dB s/n).
Selectivity: 5.5 KHz BW @ −6 dB, 20 KHz @ −40 dB.
Programming: Crystal.
Modes: AM.
Number of channels: 12
Display: LED lamp.
Search: No.

Priority: No.
Delay: Fixed.
Lock out: No.
Power source: 4.8 V DC from internal NiCads (supplied).
Audio out: 100 mW.
External connections: External Speaker, external antenna (miniature jack) and re-charge.
Manual tuning knob: No.
Dimensions: 125×71×35 mm.
Additional features: Manual step scanning for holding on any channel. Built in telescopic antenna.
Comments: Extremely compact for a 12 channel crystal controlled scanner. Dedicated set for air band only.

Model: Realistic PRO-31.
Coverage: 66–88, 138–174, 380–512.
Channels: 10.
Price: £173.87.
Comments: This is the 'cut-down' version of the PRO-33 and all details are the same except for the number of memory channels and the lack of airband.

Model: Realistic PRO-32.
Type: Hand-held portable.
All details, except for the following are identical to the 2021 model with regard to coverage, specifications and facilities.
Audio Out: 300 mW into 8 Ohms.
Power supply: 9 V DC from 6X AA cells or external adaptor.
External connections: DC, external loudspeaker and Antenna (BNC).
Dimensions: 187 H × 74 W × 45 D (mm). Weighs 550 g.
Comments: Good all-round hand held with lots of channels. The owner would be well advised though to invest in Ni-Cads and a charger. An AC adaptor is not included.

Model: Realistic PRO-2021.
Type: Synthesised Base/Mobile.
Receiver: Double Conversion Superhetrodyne (10.7/455 IF's).
Coverage: 66–88, 108–136, 138–174 and 380–512 mHz.
Sensivity: AM: 20 dB S/N @ 60% modulation = 2.0 uV. FM: 20 dB S/N @3kHz deviation: 66–88 mHz = 0.5 uV, 138–174 mHz = 1.0 uV, 380–512 mHz = 1.0 uV.
Selectivity: ± 9 kHz, −6 dB/ ±15 kHz, −50 dB.
Programming: Keypad.
Modes: Automatic selection of AM or NBFM.
Number of channels: 200 in 10 banks of 20 and 10 monitor channels.

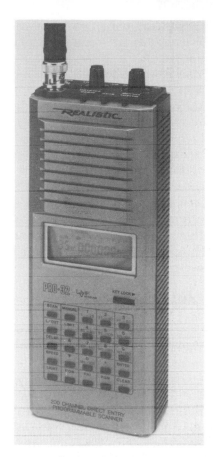

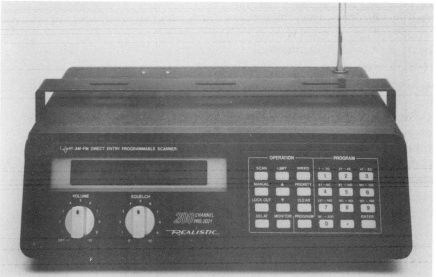

Scan/Search rate: 8 or 4 steps per second.
Display: Liquid Crystal Display (LCD) showing frequency, mode, channel, etc.
Priority: Yes. Sampled every 2 seconds.
Delay: 2 seconds.
Lock out: Yes.
Power source: 240V AC internal power supply of external 13.8v DC.
Audio out: 1 Watt into 8 Ohms.
External connections: Antenna (plug not stated), DC supply, tape outlet (phono) and External speaker.
Dimensions: 80H × 260W × 200D (mm) − 2.0kg.
Comments: Supplied with telescopic and mobile mounting bracket. Automatic AM/FM selection could be a hindrance for some users but otherwise a good budget price scanner that satisfy the needs of the user who solely wants to monitor say air band, marine and a few PMR or emergency channels.

Model: Realistic PRO-2004.
Type: Base/mobile.
Receiver: Type not stated by apparently triple-superhetrodyne.
Coverage: 25−520 and 760−1300MHz.
Quoted sensitivity: WBFM (30db S/N @ 22.5kHz Dev.).
        25–1100mHz: 3uV 1.8uV
        1100–1300mHz: 10uV
        NBFM (20dB S/N @3 kHz Dev.)
        25–520mHz 0.5uV 0.5uV
        760–1100mHz 0.3uV 0.5uV
        1100–1300mHz 3.0uV
        AM (20dB S/N @ 60% modulation)
        25–520mHz 2uV 1.7uV
        760–1100mHz 2.0uV 2.1uV
        1100–1300mHz 3.0uV
Selectivity: NFM and AM: ±9kHz @ −6dB. WFM: ±150kHz @ −6dB.
Programming: Membrane style keyboard.
Modes: Narrow AM and FM, wide FM. Mode is automatically selected according to band but can be overidden by keyboard command.
Number of channels: 300 memory channel divided into 10 banks of 30. Another 10 channels act as a 'scratch pad' to store frequencies found during searching.
Display: Liquid Crystal Display (LCD).
Search: Either in pre-determined blocks or user programmed.
Priority: User selected channel sampled every 2 seconds.
Delay:
Scan/search rate: 16 or 8 steps/channels per second.
Lock out: Programmable on any channel.

Audio out: 1.8 Watts into 8 Ohms.
Power sources: Internal AC power or external 13.8 V DC.
External connections: Antenna (BNC), tape recorder (phono), external speaker, DC power.
Dimensions: 275 W × 230 D × 75 H (mm).

Comments: Excellent value for money and at the price offers more features than some more expensive scanners. Despite the cheap'n'chearfull membrane keyboard the 2004 is very easy and fast to drive. For many months during 1987 the 2004 was not available simply because world-wide demand outstripped supply. Nothing but praise from owners.

Regency models:
These sets are sold under the Regency label but are virtually identical in most respects to the AOR series.
Importer/Agent: Garex.

Model: Regency MX5000.
Comments: Identical to the AOR 2001.
Discontinued.

Model: Regency MX7000.
Coverage: 25–550 MHz and 800 to 1300 MHz.
Comments: In most respects this set is identical to the AOR 2001. However it does have an additional frequency range of 800 to 1300 MHz and this takes in the Cellular Radio, UHF CB and Amateur 23 CM bands.

Model: Regency MX8000.
Comments: Identical to the AOR 2002.
Price: Not stated at time of writing.
Note: All Regency models are intended for the US market (110 V AC mains) and so are not supplied with a mains converter in the UK. These are available as an optional extra.

Model: Regency HX2000.
Importer/Agent: Garex.
Type: Hand held synthesised.
Coverage: 60—90, 118—175, 406—496 MHz.
Quoted sensitivity:
Programming: Key pad.
Modes: Narrow FM & AM.
Number of Channels: 20.
Display: LCD.
Search: Yes.

Priority: Yes.
Delay: Yes.
Lock out: Yes.
Power source: Internal NiCads (supplied).
Audio out: Not stated.
External connections: Not stated.
Manual tuning knob: No.
Dimensions: Not stated.
Additional features: Supplied with 'rubber duck' helical antenna, NiCad charger.

Model: Revco RS2000E.
Importer/Agent: Garex.
Type: Base/Mobile.
Receiver: Double conversion superhet.
Coverage: 60–179 MHz 380–519 MHz.
Quoted sensitivity: Not stated.
Selectivity: Not stated.
Programming: Keyboard.
Modes: AM/FM on all frequencies but not programmable (similar to the SX-200).
Number of channels: 70.
Display: LED.
Search: Yes between user defined limits.
Priority: Yes (method not stated).

Delay: Not stated.

Lock out: Yes.

Power source: 12 V or 240 V (built-in mains adaptor).

Audio out: 5 Watt.

External connections: Antenna, external speaker, tape audio, automatic tape switch.

Manual tuning knob: No.

Dimensions: 270×230×100 m.

Additional Features: Automatic storage of frequencies found whilst in search mode, transmission counter, automatic record facility.

Comments: Despite its restricted frequency range compared with say an AOR 2001, this scanner will still cover a large number of commercial and amateur allocations and it has a lot of interesting features, such as automatic search and store, that are only found on the more expensive equipment. Overall very good value for money but a small gripe in the SX-200 style 'One or the other' AM or FM mode selection.

Model: Signal R528.

Importer/Agent: Lowe.

Type: Crystal control portable.
Coverage: 118—136 MHz (Air band).
Quoted sensitivity: Better than 1.0 uV for 10 dB S+N/N.
Selectivity: 20 KHz @ 10dB.
Programming: Crystal.
Modes: Narrow AM.
Number of channels: 6.
Display: LED lamp.
Search: No.
Priority: No.
Delay: Fixed.
Lock out: No.
Power source: 9 V PP3.
Audio out: Not stated.
External connections: Antenna (BNC) and external 'speaker/headphones, 9 V DC.
Manual tuning knob: No.
Dimensions: 62×115×28 mm.
Additional features: Can be manually set to any one channel. 9 V NiCad battery with charger is available as an optional extra.
Comments: Very compact pocket portable.

Model: Signal R-532.
Importer/Agent: Lowe.
Type: Synthesised base/mobile.
Coverage: 110—136 MHz (Air band).
Quoted sensitivity: Better than 0.75 uV (10 dB S/N).
Selectivity: Not stated.
Programming: Sequential push button.
Modes: Narrow AM.
Number of Channels: 100 arranged in 10 banks of 10 with only one bank scanned at a time.
Display: LED frequency readout+LED lamps.
Search: No.
Priority: No.
Delay: Fixed.
Lock out: Yes in that only ten channels are scanned according to bank selected.
Power source: 12 V DC and memory backup (dry cells).
Audio out: Not stated.
External connections: Antenna (BNC) and external 'speaker/headphones.
Manual tuning knob: No.
Dimensions: 160×45×130 mm.

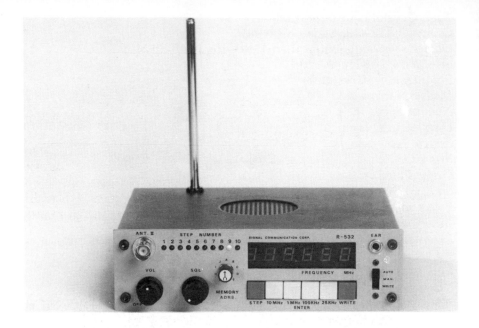

Additional features: Optional extras include: Rubber duck helical aerial, 240 V AC adaptor, NiCad battery pack with leatherette case (makes the set portable) and extension speaker.

Comments: A rugged scanner aimed solely at air band use. For a relatively high price this is a professional grade receiver.

Model: Yaesu-Musen FRG-9600.
Importer/Agent: South Midlands Communications.
Type: Synthesised base/mobile.
Receiver: Triple/Double/Single (Video) conversion.
Coverage: 60—905 MHz (no gaps).
Quoted sensitivity: FMN 0.5 uV (12 dB SINAD).
    FMW 1.0 uV (12 dB SINAD).
    AMN 1.0 uV (10 dB S+S/N).
    AMW 1.5 uV (10 dB S+S/N).
    SSB 1.0 uV (15 dB S+S/N).
Selectivity: @ 3 dB FMN 15 KHz.
    FMW 180 KHz.
    AMN 2.4 KHz.
    AMW 6.0 KHz.
    SSB 2.4 KHz.
Programming: Key pad.
Modes: Wide and narrow FM, Wide and narrow AM, SSB (up to 460 MHz only) and NTSC format video with optional adaptor.

Number of channels: 100.
Display: Green fluorescent.
Search: Yes. 100 Hz+1/5/10/12.5/25/100 KHz.
Priority: Yes.
Delay: No.
Lock out: Yes. Required channels are programmed for scan.
Power source: 12 V DC or 240 V AC via optional external adaptor. Memory backup is via rechargeable lithium cell.
Audio out: 1 Watt.
External connections: Antenna, Video out (optional), computer interface external speaker.
Manual tuning knob: Yes. Facility to transfer tuned frequency to memory and bring frequency from memory to provide a start point for manual tuning.
Dimensions: 180×80×220 mm.

Comments: Well built but it has a strange feature in that after about ten seconds it resumes scanning even if the station it stopped on is still transmitting. Various computer interfaces are available. R. Withers Communications (page 167) supply a re-vamped version with better sensitivity and UHF up to 950 mHz and, if required, an internal adaptor to give coverage from 100 kHz–60 mHz. They can also supply a PAL video adaptor.

Accessories

Listed here are some of the more exotic accessories that can be used with scanners. I have not included smaller items such as headphones, loudspeakers, slide-mounts, etc as these are generally available from a wide variety of sources including electronic hobby shops, CB dealers, etc.

Product: Revco AP2 masthead amplifier.
Distributor: Garex.
Description: A masthead pre-amplifier that gives around 18 dB of gain over the band 20–700 MHz with slightly less gain over an extended range of 10–1000 MHz. Noise figures are not quoted but the unit is very compact and has PL259 connections at either end. This means that the amplifier will easily fit inside the mounting pole of an aerial like a discone.

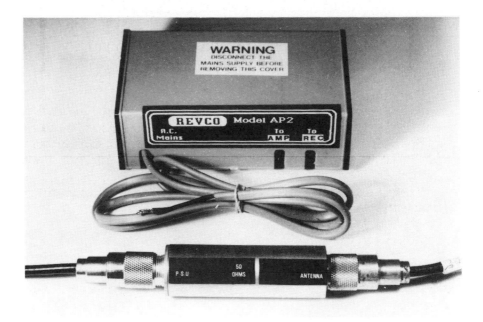

Comments: Very easy to fit. Cut into the aerial downlead just below the antenna. Fit PL259s to the cable ends and plug up to the pre-amp. If the amplifier cannot go inside the mounting pole then some kind of weather proofing will be needed such as self-amalgamating tape. At the scanner end the aerial lead is connected into the power supply box and a short lead is fitted to connect to the antenna socket of the scanner.

Product: BBA 500u Pre-amplifier.
Manufacturer: Mutek Limited.
Description: Signal pre-amplifier for use at the scanner (not masthead).
Specifications: Range   20—500 MHz
              Gain   9 dB typical.
              Noise   1.5 dB @ 100 MHz.
                      3.0 dB @ 450 MHz.
              Power   12 V DC.

Comments: Compact unit with BNC input/output connections. The price does not include the power supply but the small current drawn could easily be taken from the scanner's supply. Personally I believe the place for an amplifier is at the masthead but this unit could help boost those weaker signals for anyone not wanting to take the antenna system down to fit an amplifier.

JIL R. F. Adaptors
A range of frequency converters designed primarily for use with the SX400 Scanner but the UK Agents (Garex) say they can be used with other scanners.

RF8014: This unit covers 800 MHz to 1.4 Ghz. Its IF output lies in the range 300—500 MHz.

RF5080: This unit covers 500—800 MHz. Its IF output lies in the range 200—300 MHz.
Both units are controlled by a switching signal from the SX-400 which switches the adaptor into circuit when it is required (there is no need to start plugging or unplugging aerial and connector leads).

Connections include a 7-pin DIN plug connection to the scanner's control circuit and 12 V DC supply input.

Both converters are supplied with connecting leads, aerial plug adaptors and power supply leads and both can be brought under external computer control when the SX-400 is used in that way.

RF1030: This is an up-converter which turns the SX-400 into a fully synthesised HF communications receiver/scanner. It covers the frequency range 100 KHz to 30 MHz and has additional control circuitry as follows: Fine tuning (Delta tuning), USB, LSB and CW modes, noise blanker, AF gain, RF attenuator and squelch. The front panel also carries indicators to show band, mode and power. All operation is under full control of the main scanner.

On the back panel of the adaptor are sockets for both HF and the normal VHF/UHF aerial (automatically switched), interconnection to the scanner and 10.7 MHz IF input. This latter socket can be hooked up to the 10.7 MHz output of the scanner to give SSB operation on UHF and VHF. The adaptor contains its own independent audio output and again the whole unit can be brought under external computer control via the SX-400.

ACB300: This is an antenna control box for use with the JIL adaptors and it is a necessary accessory if more than one adaptor is going to be used. It takes the input from the normal scanner aerial plus the outputs from the adaptors and switches the appropriate circuit to the scanner. It is controlled by the SX-400's circuit. It requires 12 V DC input.

HO-1: This is a frequency converter which enables coverage of the band 96—108 MHz. Its output is in the range 26—38 MHz. It was originally designed to fill-in the gap on the SX-200 but should work with any scanner which can cover the range of its output. It has a BNC antenna socket and flying leads termninated in a Motorola plug. Power requirements are 12 V DC @ 30 mA.

Samatron U-verter

This is a British made frequency convertor which fills in the gaps on some receivers between 225 and 400 MHz. This is mostly a Military/Government allocation and within this band are the majority of military airfield spot frequencies.

The adaptor can be used with any receiver, not just scanner, that covers the range 108—136 MHz. However, when the converter is being used, all other frequencies are unobtainable. There is also a fairly complex table that has to be referred to on the front of the adaptor in order to work out what VHF frequency has to be entered in order to get

the corresponding UHF frequency (in other words the unit does not allow the user to just punch the new frequencies into his scanner).

The adaptor consists of a box of electronics with an input socket for the aerial and output to link to the aerial socket on the scanner. A 12 V DC external power source is also required although there is facility for an internal 9 V PP3 battery but this has very limited life.

The unit operates from an 18 MHz crystal controlled reference source and has a fully sealed double balanced mixer. Inputs and outputs are via Motorola type sockets. Sensitivity figures are not quoted.

Product: RTTY Terminal MPTU-1.
Manufacturer: Scarab Systems.
Description: Radioteletype interface which will connect scanners/ receivers to a wide range of computers. Suitable software must be used and Scarab can supply cassette/disc versions for the BBC, Spectrum, Commodore 64, Sinclair ZX-81 (16 k RAM needed) and the PET.
Specifications: Audio input: 10 mV minimum.
Output: 0–5 V logic level.
Baud rate: in excess of 250.
Shift: 450 Hz wide, 250 Hz narrow.
Power: 240 V AC.

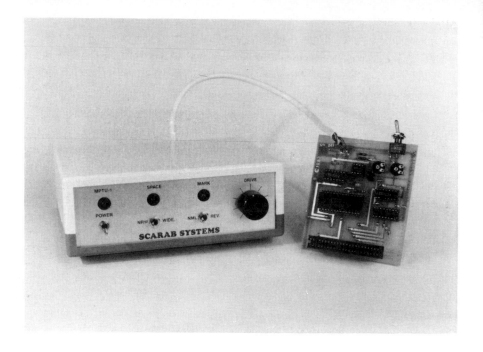

Comment: Spectrum owners will need to purchase an additional add-on board to enable the interface to be connected to the computer. Scarab can also supply a Morse interface board.

Product: Weather Station.
Manufacturer: Timestep Electronics Limited.
Description: Complete weather satellite receiving system but all individual sections can be purchased separately as follows:
Crossed Dipole (J Beam) 2X-WS
Signal pre-amplifier
Interface unit (cased)
BBC-B Software on sideways ROM
Comments: In addition, Timestep can supply single channel receivers, an SHF Meteosat converter complete with dish aerial and 64 colour level frame store. The interface unit is also available in kit form.

Antennae

I do not propose here to go into a long review of all the antennas available such as dipoles, whips, discones, etc as they are available from a wide range of sources. Instead, what are presented here are a few of the more unusual antennas which may be of interest to scanner users.

Product: Radac Antenna.

Manufacturer: Revco (available from Garex).

Description: This is what is known as a 'Nest of dipoles' type of antenna. It is quite an old idea which has been re-vamped to meet the needs of scanner users. In theory it provides reception on six bands which are determined by the length of each of the individual dipole sections. The manufacturers say that for those six bands, aerial gain will be better than a discone. Elements can be anywhere in the range 25—500 MHz.

Comments: I have had several arguments with scanner buffs over the virtues of the Radac when compared with a discone. I have never been a discone lover and believe that manufacturers make some quite outrageous claims for the performance of these devices (claiming 20 to 1300 mHz coverage for instance). My own experience with the Radac, which has been purely subjective, is that on the selected bands performance is better than a discone. If the bands are evenly spread across the spectrum then even at midway between bands performance is useable, albeit a compromise. I've owned several discones and found all

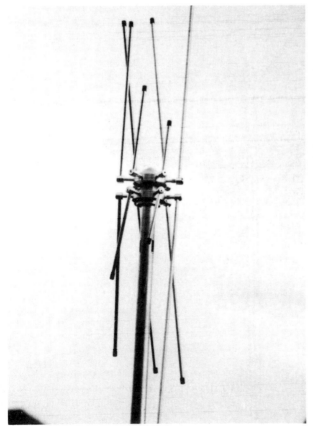

Radac Antenna

of them to have performance that falls off rapidly above 200 mHz. I suspect that although the theoretical VSWR of such devices remains relatively constant across the range some other factor, possibly radiation angle, does not. I personally prefer the nest of dipoles but will concede that the scanner owner who wants to constantly hunt all VHF/UHF frequencies may be better off with a discone.

Earlier versions of the Radac suffered from the longer elements working loose with such things as wind movement but Revco have now solved this problem by using double grub screw locking.

Product: ARA 500 Active Antenna.
Manufacturer: Dressler.
Description: Broadband antenna with built-in signal amplifier.
Gain: 50—650 MHz 17 dB typical.
        650—950 MHz 10 dB typical.

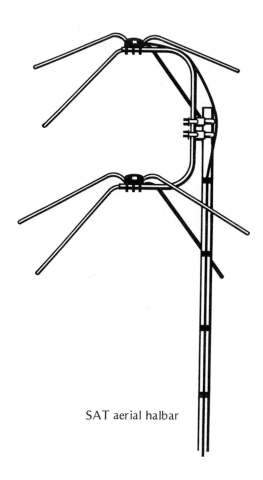

SAT aerial halbar

Noise: 1 dB @ 50—180 MHz — 1.5 dB below 300 MHz — 2.0 dB below 350 MHz —2.7 dB below 400 MHz —3.0 dB below 500 MHz — 3.8 dB below 650 MHz — 4—6 dB below 950 MHz.

Intercept: The third order intercept point is quoted as +18 dBm.

Comments: To look at it consists of a tube with bracket at the base for mounting to a mast. A broadband amplifier is built into the tube but what kind of antenna system is built into the device is not stated.

Product: I.T/u and I.T/tn Satellite antennas.

Manufacturer: Halbar.

Type: Crossed dipoles.

Description: I.T/u Covers 145.825 MHz (UOSATS 1 & 2) with left-hand circular polarisation. I.T/tn covers 137.5 weather satellite band with right hand polarisation. Both antennas have a built-in phasing harness but the purchaser must provide his own mounting mast which is not included in the price. A mast-head pre-amplifier is available for both versions and can be specified at the time of ordering so that the device can be built into the antenna.

Comments: The price of the pre-amplifier does not include a power supply. Halbar are able to supply all the equipment needed to set up a complete weather station, including receiver, digitizer and software for the BBC-B computer.

Product: Various antennas.

Agent: Tandy Corporation.

Comments: Tandy, known as Radio Shack in the USA, have been in the scanning business as long as most firms and they supply an interesting range of scanner aerials. Many of these work on the 'Trap' principle in that they have a coil part way up the vertical element so making them resonant at UHF and VHF. For Mobile operation in particular this can mean better performance than just a straightforward whip aerial.

Model: 20—018. Trapped vertical whip with magnetic mount base and cable.

Model: 20—161. Trapped vertical whip with Motorola right angled plug at the base for direct connection to the scanner. This should be better than a simple telescopic for people who cannot or will not fit an external aerial.

Model: 20—014. Base aerial 'Nest of Dipoles' type arrangement but with horizontal ground planes for UHF and 2 VHF bands.

Model: 20—017. Mobile 'no-hole' mounting, trapped whip complete with cable.

Model: 20—9005. UHF/VHF base antenna. To look at it is a slim plastic pole which contains the elements. Internal arrangements are not stated. *Comment:* It was not possible to obtain pictures of these antennas but they are shown in the Tandy Catalogue available from hundreds of stores around Britain.

Main importers/ 10 manufacturers/agents

Names and addresses

AERO HOBBY SUPPLIES
Hangar Road, Birmingham International Airport (Cargo),
West Midlands B26 3QJ
Telephone 021-742 8704

GAREX ELECTRONICS
7 Norvic Road, Marsworth, Tring, Hertfordshire HP23 4LS
Telephone: 0296 668684
Comment: Garex are linked with Revco and are the main retail outlet for
Revco's products.

LOWE ELECTRONICS LIMITED
Chesterfield Road, Matlock, Derbyshire DE4 5LE
Telephone (0629) 2817, 2430, 4057, 4995

REVCO ELECTRONICS LIMITED
Poundwell Street, Modbury, South Devon PL21 0RQ
Telephone: 0548–830 665

RADIO SHACK LIMITED
188 Broadhurst Gardens, London NW6 3AY
Telephone: 01-624 7174

SOUTH MIDLANDS COMMUNICATIONS LIMITED
SM House, Rumbridge Street, Totton, Southampton SO4 4DP
Telephone: 0703 867333

TANDY CORPORATION
Tandy products are sold through franchised dealers. A store stocking
Tandy products will be found in most towns and cities (try the yellow
pages or the telephone directory). However, in case of difficulty in
finding a dealer, Tandy do have a central office which can be contacted as
a last resort.

TANDY CORPORATION
(Branch UK), Tameway Tower, Bridge Street, Walsall,
West Midlands WS1 1LA

THANET ELECTRONICS LIMITED
Sea Street, Herne Bay, Kent
Telephone: 0227 363859

Equipment dealers
These dealers supply scanning equipment on a mail order basis and
most have export facilities.

AMATEUR ELECTRONICS
504 Alum Rock Road, Alum Rock, Birmingham B8 3HX
Telephone: 021–327 1497/6313

AMCOMM SERVICES LIMITED
194 Northolt Road, South Harrow, Middlesex HA2 0EN
Telephone: 01-422 9585

A.R.E. COMMUNICATIONS LIMITED
38 Bridge Street, Earlestown, Newton-Le-Willows, Merseyside
Telephone: 09252-29881

BREDHURST ELECTRONICS
High Street, Handcross, West Sussex RH17 6BW
Telephone: 0444-400786

CIRKIT HOLDINGS LIMITED
Park Lane, Broxbourne, Hertfordshire EN10 7NQ
Telephone: 0992-444111
(Pre-amp and BFO kits, plugs, sockets, only)

DRESSLER (UK) LIMITED
191 Francis Road, Leyton, London E10
Telephone 01-558 0854

HALBAR LIMITED
Unit 1, Bury Walk, Bedford MK41 0DU
Telephone: 0234 44720
(Satellite aerials, hardware and software)

MAPLIN ELECTRONIC SUPPLIES LIMITED
P.O. Box 3, Rayleigh, Essex SS6 8LR
Telephone: 0702 552991
(Plugs, components, weather satellite digitizer)

MUTEK LIMITED
Bradworthy, Holsworthy, Devon EX22 7TU
Telephone: 040-924 543(Pre-amps only)

PHOTO ACOUSTICS LIMITED
58 High Street, Newport Pagnell, Buckinghamshire MK16 8AQ
Telephone: 0908 610625

REG. WARD AND COMPANY LIMITED
1 Western Parade, West Street, Axminister, Devon EX13 5NY
Telephone: 0297 34918

SCARAB SYSTEMS LIMITED
39 Stafford Street, Gillingham, Kent ME7 5EN
Telephone: 0634 570441
(RTTY/CW/SSTV hardware and software only)

STEPHEN JAMES LIMITED
47 Warrington Road, Leigh, Lancs WN7 3EA
Telephone: 0942 676790

TELECOMMS
189 London Roads, Portsmouth, Hampshire PO2 9AE
Telephone: 0705 662145

TIMESTEP ELECTRONICS LIMITED
Agents are: GAREX
(Weather satellite adaptors and software)

WATERS AND STANTON
18-20 Main Road, Hockley, Essex
Telephone: 0702 206835

Organisations
AMATEUR RADIO

THE RADIO SOCIETY OF GREAT BRITAIN
Lambda House, Cranborne Road, Potters Bar,
Hertfordshire EN6 3JW
Telephone: 0707 59015

MARINE, LAND MOBILE, ETC, GOVERNMENT REGULATORY
BODY

THE DEPARTMENT OF TRADE AND INDUSTRY
Radio Regulatory Division (R1), Waterloo Bridge House, Waterloo
Road, London SE1 8UA

11 Scanners 2

Scanners 2 is the perfect match to the book you are reading now. It is not just a revised version of Scanners 1 but an entirely separate book that goes into the subject of the more advanced scanner user and also covers VHF/UHF monitor receivers. Scanners 2 is also an international edition.

Here are some of the subjects that are covered:

Modifications: Simultaneous AM/FM for the SX-200 and Bearcat 220FB.

Common faults: SX-200 (various improvements), Bearcat 220 (power supply), AOR 2001 (Off frequency), etc.

DIY accessories: Active antenna, SX-200 front panel S-Meter, B.F.O., broadband and narrow band masthead amplifiers, power supplies, auto NiCad charger, 12 V to 6 V or 9 V adaptor for portables and automatic recording switch.

Project: Build a 10 channel crystal controlled pocket or mobile scanner. Easy to build VHF/FM design that uses parts available from regular component suppliers.

Computer control: A detailed look at the advantages of using a personal computer to control a scanner (AOR 2002, ICOM, SX–400, etc.).

Dxing: Using your scanner for long distance reception. How to recognise the signs that a lift is on, where to tune and hear stations from as far away as the USA under the right conditions. List of VHF broadcast stations, beacons, repeaters, etc.

Spectrum: Full international spectrum allocations for all three ITU regions from 26–1300 MHz.

Callsigns: Full list of International Air and Marine Callsigns and registrations.

LOGBOOK

Mem No.	Fcy MHz	Mode	Station	Notes
01				
02				
03				
04				
05				
06				
07				
08				
09				
10				
11				
12				
13				
14				
15				
16				
17				
18				
19				
20				

LOGBOOK

Mem No.	Fcy MHz	Mode	Station	Notes
21				
22				
23				
24				
25				
26				
27				
28				
29				
30				
31				
32				
33				
34				
35				
36				
37				
38				
39				
40				

LOGBOOK

Mem No.	Fcy MHz	Mode	Station	Notes

LOGBOOK

Mem No.	Fcy MHz	Mode	Station	Notes

Index

Abbreviations, 130
Accessories, 67—76, 156—161
Active antennas, 66, 162
AFC (automatic frequency control), 28
AF scan, 26
Air band, 12, 18, 81, 84—94
Air force, 88—91, 124
Air traffic control, 84—94, 125—133
Airways, 128—130
Alternator whine, 43
Amateur bands, 19, 98—103
Amateur callsigns, 118—121
Amplitude Modulation (AM), 12, 31
Amplifiers, 66, 156—157
AMSAT, 114
ANL (automatic noise limiter), 28
Antennas, 47—66, 161—164
Antenna amplifiers, 66, 156—157
Antenna switches, 75
Approach control, 84—91, 127, 128
ASCCI code, 18
Astronauts, 112
ATIS (airport terminal information service), 87, 131
Attenuator, 32
Audio frequency, 5, 16, 33
Auto-write scan, 28
Aviation bands, 84—94
Aviation callsigns, 125
Aviation RT procedure, 125—132

Band plans, 77—106
Bandwidth, 13, 25, 28
Base leg, 129
Base station, 37
Basic radio theory, 5—21
Batteries, 24, 42, 68
BFO (beat Frequency oscillator), 14, 17
Birdies, 26
BNC plug, 56, 60
Body mount aerials, 49
Bonding, 44

British airfield frequencies, 84—91
Broadband antennas, 47, 55, 161—164
Broadband television, 17
Building an aerial, 62

C.A.A. (Civil Aviation Authority), 3
Cables, 58
Calling channel, 94
Callsigns, 118—121, 122, 125
Capacitors, 24
Carphone, 81, 104, 107
Carrier squelch, 26
Carrier wave, 5,11
CB (citizens band), 12, 110—111
Cellular radio, 81, 104, 107
Channelising, 15, 95
Channel separation, 15, 25
Charging (cells), 41, 68
Chimney lashing kits, 65
Circuit (airfield), 127, 129
Circuit diagrams, 38
Circular polarisation, 49, 163
Citizens band, 110—111
Civilian airfield frequencies, 84—86
Clear, 29
Coastal Command, 124
Coastal stations, 97
Coastguard, 93, 124
Coaxial Cable, 51, 58
Communications satellites, 112—116
Company frequencies, 87, 130
Compulsory reporting point, 128
Computers, 17, 18, 34, 71—74, 160—161
Connectors, 33, 60
Contest stations, 120—121
Controlled airspace, 128
Control tower, 36, 84—94
Converters (frequency), 74, 158—159
Cordless 'phones, 81
Cosmonauts, 112, 115
Crossed dipole, 57, 59, 113, 163
Crystal calculations, 38

Crystal control, 22, 38
CW (Morse), 11, 16, 71

DC supplies, 41, 67
Dead zone, 10
Delay (squelch), 27
Demodulators, 6, 14
Department of Trade and Industry, 3, 167
Detectors, 6, 12,
Deviation, 13
Deviation muting, 26
Dimensions (aerials), 51, 63
Dial, 29, 31
Dipoles, 52, 62
Directional aerials, 52, 53
Discones, 54
Discriminator, 14
Distances, 8, 87, 94, 104
Distress frequencies, 77—81, 92, 124
Doppler shift, 28, 113
Downlink frequencies, 113
Downwind leg, 129
Duplex, 18, 95

Eaves mounting kits, 65
EHF (extremely high frequency), 7
E-layer, 9
Emergency frequencies, 92, 108—109, 124
Enter, 29
Envelope (modulation), 12

Fast scan television, 17, 103
FAX (facsimile), 17
Final approach, 127
Fine tune, 29
F-layers, 9
Flight clearance, 128
Flight Information, 130
Flight plan, 128
Flutter, 44
Folded dipole, 53
Frequency, 5, 77—116
Frequency converters, 74, 158—159
Frequency stepping, 23
FM (frequency modulation), 12, 31
Full tuning, 29

Generator whine, 43
Government regulations, 2, 5
Ground handling, 127
Ground plane, 49
Ground wave, 8
Guard band, 16
Gutter mounts, 49

Half duplex, 21
Headphones, 68—70
Helical aerials, 39, 56
HF (high frequency), 7
Horizontal polarization, 48, 52
Hysteresis, 28

IF (intermediate frequency), 34, 39
Ignition noise, 42
In-line choke, 43
Inputs, 33
Interference, 28, 41
Ionosphere, 9
Irish airfield frequencies, 84—86
ISM (industrial, scientific, medical), 81
ITU (international Telecommunication Union),
    77, 83

Keyboards, 3, 23
Key lock, 30

Land mobile, 14, 103—112
LARS (lower airspace radar service), 130
Layers (E, F1, F2), 9
Legal requirements, 2
LF (low frequency), 7
Licences, 2
Lifeboats, 93, 94, 124
Lift conditions, 11
Link calls, 94—97
Locators, 82
Lock-out, 30, 36
Loudspeakers, 68
Lower sideband, 15

Magnetic aerial mounts, 40, 49
Mains adaptor, 41, 67
Manual key, 30
Marine bands, 14, 21, 94—98
Marine RT procedure, 122—125
Mast, 65
Masthead amplifier, 66, 156
MATZ (military aerodrome traffic zone), 88—91,
    130
Mayday calls, 124—125
Memories, 23
Memory count, 30
Memory scanning, 36
Message handling, 108
Meteor scatter, 101
Meteosat, 115
MF (medium frequency), 7
Military, 88—91, 115, 126
Miniature jack plug, 61, 68
Mobile aerials, 49, 164
Mobile operation, 37, 42, 74

Mobile satellite service, 82, 115
Model control, 25, 82
Modes (AM—FM, SSB), 6, 11, 31
Mode selector, 31
Moonbounce, 101
Morse code, 11, 16, 71
Motorola plug, 61
Mounting kits, 64
Multi-hop, 10
Mute, 25

Narrow band antennas, 47, 49
NBFM (narrow band FM), 29
NASA shuttle, 72, 112—116
NATO, 93
Navigation beacons, 18, 89, 93, 112
Navigation warnings, 123
Navy, 124
NOAA satellites, 115

On-site paging, 82, 107—108
Operating, 35
Ordering crystals, 38
Oscar satellites, 114
Output sockets, 33

Pagers, 82, 107—108
Pan calls, 118
PAR (precision approach radar), 91, 127—128
Phonetic alphabet, 117
PL259 plug, 60
Plymouth rescue centre, 93
PMR (private mobile radio), 12, 24, 104—106
Polarity, 41, 48, 57
Polar orbiting satellites, 73
Portables, 38, 56
Port operations, 96, 124
Power converters, 40
Power supplies, 40, 67—68
Power (transmitter), 5
Pre-set squelch, 27
Priority, 31
Private mobile radio, see PMR
Programming, 23, 45
Propagation, 8—11
Public radiophones, 96, 104, 107

Q codes, 119
QFE, 126, 127, 128
QNH, 132
Quarter wave whips, 48—51
Quartz crystals, 22, 38

Radio microphones, 82
Radionavigation, 18, 89, 93, 112

Radiophones, 21, 81, 104, 107
Radio theory, 5—21
R.A.F., 88—91, 124
RAYNET, 99
Receivers (theory), 5—21
Rechargeable batteries, 41, 68
Repeaters, 19, 100, 101, 102, 112, 122
Reporting codes, 120
Rescue services, 92, 108—109, 124
RF amplifier, 66, 156—157
Rotators, 54
RS232 interface, 34
RSGB (Radio Society of Great Britain), 3, 167
RS satellites, 114
RST code, 120
RT procedure, 117—132
RTTY (radio teletype), 17, 71—74, 160—161
Rubber duck aerials, 39, 56

SARBE, 82, 92
Salyut, 112, 115
Satellite aerials, 57, 59, 112, 113, 163
Satellite frequencies, 101, 112—116
Satellite navigation, 82, 112
Scan-A, Scan B, 36
Scanner tricks, 45
Scan rate, 32
Scene of search, 93
Search and rescue, 81, 93
Searching, 23, 35
Search stop, 32
Securité, 123
SHF (Super high frequency), 7
Ship-to-ship, 95, 124
Ship-to-shore, 95, 124
Shuttle (NASA), 72, 112, 115
Signal booster, 66, 156—157
Signal meter, 32, 120
Simplex, 18, 95—96
Skip, 10
Skywave, 8
Slant polarisation, 49
Slide mount, 38, 74
Slope detection, 14, 29
Slow scan television, 17, 72—74
Software, 71—74
Solar effects, 10
Space satellites, 112—116
Special event stations, 112
Spectrum 6—8, 77—81
Split frequency simplex, 18
Sporadic-E, 98
Squelch, 25
Squelch delay, 27
SRA (surveillance radar approach), 91, 127—128
SSB (single sideband) 14, 29, 34, 98—103
Standard frequency, 82
Startup procedure, 128
Stepping, 32

Step rate, 32
Suppressors, 41
Switches, 25
Switching control, 33
Synthesised scanners, 22, 23, 35

Talkthrough, 20
Telecontrol, 82
Telemetry, 18
Telescopic aerials, 39, 47, 56
Television, 58, 82
Time, 118
Traffic lists, 122
Transmission (types), 16—18
Transmitters (theory), 5
Transmitting blind, 118
Transponding, 113
Tropospherical ducting, 8, 10, 98

UHF (ultra high frequency), 7
UIR (upper information region), 130
UK frequency allocations, 77—116
UOSAT, 113
Uplink frequencies, 113

Upper sideband, 15
USAF, 88—90

Vehicle interference, 41
Vertical polarisation, 48, 52
VFR (visual flight rules), 128
VHF (very high frequency), 7
VLF (very low frequency), 7
Voice squelch, 26
VOMETS, 87, 93
Voltage converters, 40
Vox (voice operated switching), 21

Wavelength, 6—8
Weather (effects on radio), 5, 11
Weather forecasts, 123
Weather Satellites, 71—74, 82, 114—115, 161
Whip aerials, 48—51, 164
Wide area paging, 82, 107
Wireless Telegraphy Act, 2

Yagi aerials, 52—53

AR2002 . . . . . The AOR AR2002 is a high
performance monitor receiver covering
frequencies from 25 to 550 and 800 to 1300 MHz.
Frequency stepping is by keypad or knob in
selectable increments of 5, 12.5 or 25 kHz steps.
Modes of operation are AM, narrow band FM and
wide band FM. The AR2002 has twenty memory
channels and a comprehensive range of scanning
and search facilities. A front panel liquid crystal
display shows frequency, mode, channel number,
frequency increment, delay engaged etc. Operating
from 12 volts DC the receiver can be used mobile (a
mains power supply is included with each AR2002
for home use together with a simple aerial).

A socket on the rear panel enables the optional
RS232 interface (RC PACK) to be connected to the
AR2002. Linked to a suitable computer the
interface greatly increases the facilities enjoyed by
the AR2002 owner. For those owning one of the
popular BBC computers, we have produced a
plug-in EPROM (ARPROM) which will save you
having to write your own programme.

AR2002

LOWE ELECTRONICS LIMITED

Chesterfield Road, Matlock, Derbyshire DE4 5LE
Telephone 0629 2817, 2430, 4057, 4995   Telex 377482 LOWLEC G
Sole authorised importer and distributer for AOR and SIGNAL equipment

R528 . . . . . The SIGNAL R528 is a pocket-sized airband receiver scanning four out of six crystal controlled channels (crystals not included). This feature enables frequencies where transmission is continuous, such as VOLMET and ATIS, to be placed in positions five and six where they will not affect the scanning function. As an alternative to scanning, channels can also be selected manually by push button. The R528 operates from an internal 9 volt battery (PP3). An optional nicad battery (RX22) and charger (CH122) are available and for listening at home a mains power supply (PS9) can be plugged into the receiver. The SIGNAL R528 is supplied with an earpiece, flexible aerial, dry battery and instructions for use.

R532 . . . . . Not needing crystals, the SIGNAL R532 is a synthesized receiver covering the airbands from 110 to 136 MHz. The required frequencies are easily written into the receiver and can be entered into any of the one hundred memories (ten banks of ten). Once the memories are programmed, manual selection of the appropriate tower, radar or approach frequency is simple. So that no transmission is missed, the R532 will scan any one of the ten memory banks, holding while a frequency is busy. One of the advantages of synthesized equipment is that new frequencies can be written over the old ones. Operating on 12 volts DC, the R532 can be used in your car or at home with the optional mains adapter (PS12). For total self-contained flexibility, a nicad pack complete with carrying case (LCPB532), a mains charger (CH532) and a top mounted telescopic whip aerial (BNC6) are available as optional extras.

To further improve reception at home, both the R528 and R532 airband receivers can be used with external aerials and for mobile operation aerials suitable for your car are also available.

R528

R532

LOWE ELECTRONICS LIMITED

Chesterfield Road, Matlock, Derbyshire DE4 5LE
Telephone 0629 2817, 2430, 4057, 4995   Telex 377482 LOWLEC G
Sole authorised importer and distributer for AOR and SIGNAL equipment

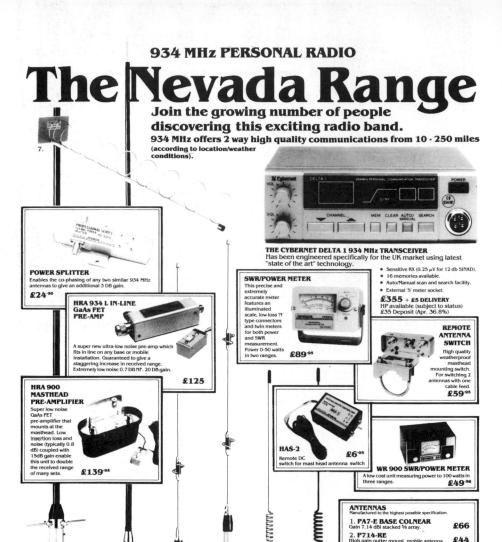

ICOM

IC·R7000, 25-2000MHz

Commercial quality scanning receiver

ICOM introduces the IC-R7000 advanced technology continuous coverage communications receiver. With 99 programmable memories the IC-R7000 covers CB, Aircraft, Marine, FM broadcast, Amateur Radio, Television and weather satellite bands. For simplified operation and quick tuning the IC-R7000 features direct keyboard entry. Precise frequencies can be selected by pushing the digit keys in sequence of the frequency or by turning the main tuning knob. FM wide/FM narrow/AM,Iupper and lower SSB modes with six tuning speeds: .1, 1.0, 5, 10, 12.5, 25KHz. The IC-R7000 has 99 memories available to store your favourite frequencies including the operating mode. Memory channels can be called up by pressing memory switch then rotating the memory channel knob or by direct keyboard entry.

A sophisticated scanning system provides instant access to the most used frequencies. By depressing the auto-M switch, the IC-R7000 automatically memorises frequencies that are in use whilst it is in the scan mode. This allows you to recall frequencies that were in use. The scanning speed is adjustable and the scanning system includes memory selected frequency ranges or priority channels. All functions including memory channel readout are clearly shown on a dual colour fluorescent display.

Other features includes dial lock, noise blanker, attenuator, display dimmer and S meter, and optional RC-12 infra-red remote controller, voice synthesizer and HP1 headphones. For more details of the IC-R7000 and other ICOM radio equipment contact Thanet Electronics and we will be able to help you.

Thanet Electronics
Sea Street, Herne Bay, Kent. CT6 8LD.
Tel: (0227) 363859.

 *Electronics Today International* is Britain's leading magazine for the electronics enthusiast and is renowned for its ability to keep pace with the leading edge of technology. Offering both practical and theoretical examples, in the form of DIY projects and detailed technical explanations, it provides a single-source guide to tomorrow's microchip world. *Electronics Today International* is published monthly.

Electronics and computer enthusiasts have a constant requirement for information about their subject. *Electronics Digest* provides 100

ELECTRONICS DIGEST

pages of relevant, but hard to obtain, data in every issue. The theme for an issue might be constructional projects, or component data, or digital logic or indeed anything within the broad spectrum of the subject. Whatever it is, *Electronics Digest* covers it in-depth and provides an invaluable reference source in a convenient magazine format. *Electronics Digest* is published quarterly.

 As the CB craze died away, the number of people wanting to become full radio amateurs increased dramatically. A large percentage of these are young people, unserved by the traditionally staid magazines in the field. *Ham Radio Today* is the magazine to help. It covers all aspects of this growing field and does so in a lively and entertaining manner. *Ham Radio Today* is published monthly.

TAKE OUT THE UNCERTAINTY...
...TAKE OUT A SUBSCRIPTION

	ELECTRONICS TODAY INTERNATIONAL	ELECTRONICS DIGEST	HAM RADIO TODAY
U.K.	£18.10	£11.30	£17.30
Overseas Surface Mail	£22.50 $29.50 (U.S.)	£14.00 $18.00 (U.S.)	£21.00 $28.00 (U.S.)
Overseas Airmail	£49.50	£23.00	£39.00

If you would like to subscribe to any of these magazines, please make your cheque, postal order or international money order payable to ARGUS SPECIALIST PUBLICATIONS LTD, or send your Access/Barclaycard number to the following address or telephone your credit card order on 0442 48432.

Send your remittance to:
INFONET LTD., Times House, 179 The Marlowes, Hemel Hempstead, Herts. HP1 1BB.